COOKING
WITH HERB

COOKING
WITH HERB

75 RECIPES FOR THE
MARLEY NATURAL LIFESTYLE

CEDELLA MARLEY

WITH RAQUEL PELZEL

PHOTOGRAPHS BY AUBRIE PICK

PAM KRAUSS BOOKS / AVERY
NEW YORK

an imprint of Penguin Random House LLC
375 Hudson Street
New York, New York 10014

Library of Congress Cataloging-in-Publication Data

Names: Marley, Cedella, author. | Pelzel, Raquel, author.
Title: Marley Natural : a guide to the cannabis lifestyle, with 75
   herb-boosted recipes / by Cedella Marley with Raquel Pelzel.
Description: New York : Pam Krauss Books/Avery, [2017] | Includes
   bibliographical references and index.
Identifiers: LCCN 2016058536 (print) | LCCN 2017002712 (ebook) | ISBN
   9780553496444 (alk. paper) | ISBN 9780553496451 (ebook)
Subjects: LCSH: Cooking (Marijuana) | Marley Natural. | LCGFT: Cookbooks.
Classification: LCC TX819.M25 M253 2017 (print) | LCC TX819.M25 (ebook) | DDC 641.3/03—dc23
LC record available at https://lccn.loc.gov/2016058536
p.   cm.

Printed in China
10 9 8 7 6 5 4 3 2 1

Book design by Ashley Tucker

CONTENTS

INTRODUCTION 9
THE NEW WORLD OF HERB 15
COOKING THE MARLEY WAY 33
ENHANCED DINNER PARTIES: ENTERTAINING WITH HERB 53

1
GOOD MORNING JAH
61

2
ANYTIME QUENCHERS
81

3
ALL-DAY MUNCHIES!
99

4
FRESH AND GREEN
121

5
THE GET-TOGETHER
137

6
SWEETS THAT SATISFY
189

7
NATURAL BEAUTY
213

MARLEY FAMILY FOOD PRODUCTS 229

ACKNOWLEDGMENTS 230

INDEX 233

INTRODUCTION

"When you smoke the herb, it reveals you to yourself."
—BOB MARLEY

*"As we feel peaceful, I generate energy of peace.
Where there was stress, there is now calm."*
—CEDELLA MARLEY

WHEN YOU THINK OF BOB MARLEY you probably think of the Herb, cannabis (in my family, we just call it *Herb*). Growing up, I was always surrounded by it—for me, the sweet whiff was as common as the aroma of Mommy burning the ginger and curry together in coconut oil for one of her famous one-pot stews. From the time Daddy was a small boy he always respected nature and the healing properties of plants. His grandfather Omeriah was an herbalist and farmer and Daddy told stories about his grandfather grinding on "chewstick," a natural, wild-growing vine with antiseptic and antibacterial properties that was used as a natural toothpaste in Jamaica. He was also known for his "elixirs" that cleansed, restored, and balanced the mind, blood, and soul. When Daddy embraced the Rastafari way of life in the mid-1960s, the philosophy of living in peace and love, and being mindful of what you put in your body, resonated with the teachings and experiences of his upbringing. herb is sacramental for Rastafarians and is even referenced in the Bible. Daddy smoked to put himself in a joyous, holy, and inspirational

OPPOSITE: Mommy, Sharon, Ziggy, Stephen (in the stroller), and me (with my favorite purse!) with Daddy

mind-set, to free his spirit and creativity. Now, more than thirty years after my father left this earth, the world is finally opening up to the many benefits of the Herb, from the relief of constant pain to opening creative pathways.

My relationship with my parents was always great, and today, my mother is my best friend. Of course having only had thirteen years with my father, I will always wish I'd had more time with him. Still I am blessed to have the memories I do have of our family, of simply hanging out, swimming, running on the beach, and enjoying fresh juices, great food, and music. I am forever grateful to my parents for showing us how to appreciate the slower pace of life, to think critically and live healthfully, and "apprecilove" the beauty and bounty of Mother Earth. My mother showed us how to live from the garden and cook delicious food, and this book is a way for me to share my family's legacy with the world, as a testament to both of them and as an antidote to our high-pressured lives. Living as one with nature, music, and the Herb helps spread a message of love and unity, health, and happiness and positive vibrations all around.

Growing up, having Herb in my life was pretty normal. That's just the way it was. My parents didn't smoke to get silly, they smoked to connect with their deepest and truest selves. When Dad smoked, he'd sit and read his Bible, write lyrics, and take a draw here and there off his spliff. For my parents, smoking was a sacred ritual, and they respected the power of the Herb. So as a young woman it seemed perfectly natural to incorporate Herb into my lifestyle, whether for strictly recreational purposes or to relieve painful cramps or to come down from the natural high of being on stage, and frankly, sometimes just to chill. There are many reasons why people smoke—creative inspiration, to ease aches and pains, to calm anxieties. It's not always to be one with the Universe, though some may achieve that as well. Some folks just get lit. Hey . . . do you?

Like Mommy, I eventually stopped smoking to take care of my voice. For singers, smoking of any kind isn't a great thing to do on a regular basis. But Herb and its hemp by-products will always be a part of my lifestyle because of their many beneficial qualities, especially when taken in edible form, where smoke inhalation is not an issue.

Cooking with Herb is by no means a new way to experience its psychological and medicinal benefits—people have been using it this way forever, let's just get real! It's only recently that Herb was villainized . . . and now that it can finally come out of the closet (at least in some states), we can all re-educate ourselves about what this wondrous plant

CLOCKWISE FROM TOP RIGHT: With Grandma Cedella Booker and Mommy (Rita Marley); with my son Skip; with my namesake, Grandma Cedella; Daddy.

can do for us. In this book you'll find not just recipes but ways, time, and guidance for cooking with and experiencing the Herb to its greatest potential—from teas and tonics to soups and soaks. For uplifting your spirit, entertaining and having fun with your friends, and for your health, Herb can be a part of your kitchen pantry from breakfast through late-night munching (and in the Marley house, munchies are not chips and cereal).

There's a lot to know about Herb scientifically, and I've looked to the Marley Natural team of experts for information on what to ask when buying Herb, how best to unlock the THC, and the best ways to incorporate Herb into food. Because while I have grown up with Herb in my life, I'm by no means a scientist. There's so much to learn and know, and now that Herb is becoming more accepted and better regulated, we can all look forward to more discoveries about Herb's numerous benefits for body, mind, and spirit.

I hope you find ways to explore the Herb in your cooking, have fun with it, host parties where everyone is open, uplifted, and feeling *irie* . . . it's truly a beautiful thing! Herb (and this book) should not be misused. The last thing I want (unless you want it!) is to bring you to a place where all you can do is sit on the sofa and stare at the wall. It's to bring new energy to your gatherings, help unlock your creative side, and lend a balance of quiet contemplation to daily life—your yoga practice, hikes, bike rides, and meditations. Cooking is a lifelong journey of providing joy to your people . . . Herb can only enhance that joy, and make it all the more lovely. My daddy used to say that "Herb is the unification of mankind." Now *that* is a beautiful vision.

In peace and with love,

Cedella Marley

"If you want to be helpful, be happy. If you want to be successful, be happy. Happiness is not the result of a life well lived. Happiness is the fuel for a life well lived. If you won't let yourself be happy, you can't be happy. Yet when you simply allow happiness, nothing can keep it from you."

THE NEW WORLD OF HERB

LET'S JUST CUT TO THE CHASE HERE: Herb is no longer a four-letter word. State after state is legalizing the use of Herb, and so many are rethinking its value as a source for better health, both physically and spiritually; it's not just about the high. Some may have experienced the medicinal benefits of Herb for pain management, epilepsy, eye health, anxiety, post-traumatic stress syndrome, and more. Hemp seeds (usually when used for manufacturing purposes the seeds have THC levels that are negligible or non-existent) can be made into a myriad of products from fabric to paper, the seeds can be used to add texture to food or pressed for their oil, while the plant itself (Herb, not hemp) can be made into topical ointments, can be juiced, or dried and smoked. When you think about it, Herb is a natural mystic—humans are in fact born with endocannibinoid receptors, biological receptors in the brain and elsewhere whose specific function is to receive the good and healing properties of Herb. As legalization of the Herb expands, more of its benefits will be revealed and we will certainly unlock even more ways in which this plant that grows in nature is beneficial for our mind, body, and spirit.

Even though my father was a private person, he smoked freely and without fear. He once said, "I man, a farmer, since creation," so I know without question that he would have loved to witness the legalization of Herb and the movement of acceptance among the medical community as well as those who just want to chill out and relax and use Herb as a way to enlightenment. There are so many beneficial uses for this plant, and its side effects, so inconsequential compared to other man-made medicines (and intoxicants), it is just plain stupid that something natural and from the earth like the Herb has been illegal for so long . . . or maybe it's political (let's not even go there!). The ways that my family uses Herb are as diverse and varied as the colors of the ocean. It is really a part of the fabric of our lives—we steep it into tea, infuse it into oil or butter for cooking, juice the raw leaves, grind the dried flower into a spice blend, or we infuse creams and oils to make a medicated or nonmedicated topical treatment for the skin (hemp oil is an incredible moisturizer).

We use Herb to bring us closer to our spiritual selves, to chill out, and of course to have fun. You can infuse your morning green juice with Herb and go for a hike or run, you can pair wine with Herb for a dinner party, you can use Herb to calm achy muscles or add an Herb-spiked tincture to your bath for a spa-worthy relaxing experience. Herb doesn't have to be used under cover anymore—it can become a part of your life, as much as cooking, exercise, and entertaining are.

The Herb has been on earth since the beginning of time. Now that it is legal and acceptable in more places, consumers can be picky about what they buy, how it is grown, and who grew it. Although people have been growing it in secret and in dark rooms under artificial light or in closets for decades, like any crop, Herb thrives in fresh air and with ample sunlight. Now that the recreational use of Herb is legal in some states and others allow it to be used medicinally, the methods for growing it are constantly improving. Family farmers can feel confident and secure cultivating Herb out in the open.

Smoking Herb just like my parents did is still probably the most popular way to use it, but I like to incorporate it into foods using Herb-infused butters and oils (see page 17 for all the details). Enhancing a dish with some CannaButter or CannaOil turns an ordinary dinner with friends into an immediate celebration of life and feeling good. It's a really wonderful way to entertain, and put everyone into a higher vibration . . . yeah man. I mean imagine a party where everyone just forgets their troubles and dances! Enhancing dishes with Herb is a way to make everyone feel *irie* and mellow, just as you might offer them a cocktail or a glass of wine. (See pages 53–57 for more information about putting together an enhanced menu for entertaining.)

If you have unpleasant memories of eating food enhanced with cannabis—perhaps you tried a pot brownie when you were younger—no doubt the item in question was made simply by tossing a handful of dried Herb into the mix. If that was the case, and especially if the Herb used was of low potency and poor quality, you'll find cooking with

MARLEY NATURAL HERB AND OIL

The members of my family all are big believers in the health benefits of Herb (see page 21)—its healing powers and ability to awaken our inner well-being—even if some of us choose not to smoke. My family launched Marley Natural as a global brand in 2014 as a way to honor my father's legacy. When Herb is sold under the Marley Natural brand, you can be sure the Herb is all natural and sustainably harvested as nature intended. We source the highest quality premium flowers grown sustainably by experienced growers and without fertilizers, pesticides, or chemicals. We take pride in offering select genetics and heirloom strains of Herb, with the Marley Natural line including Marley Green, a hybrid sativa/indica blend, Marley Gold, a sativa-dominant strain, Marley Red, a high-CBD strain (page 21), and Marley Black, an indica-dominant strain.

Our Herb oil (a concentrated and very pure extraction of Herb) is extracted from the flowers with care to preserve the fullest spectrum of the plant's natural terpene profile. The oil is extracted using a combination of pressure, heat, and carbon dioxide to separate the plant material. Advanced refining techniques remove impurities and concentrate the cannabinoid profile of the oil. Of course both our Herb and oil are tested for purity and safety. It is part of the Rastafarian lifestyle—to live in peace and love, and to put only positive things into your body to create a better life for yourself and others. This philosophy was important to my father, and it remains important to our family when it comes to anything we put in or on our body.

HOW OUR BODY
USES HERB AS MEDICINE

Herb is a wondrous plant. It contains more than eighty different cannabinoids that interact in various ways with the human body's endocannibinoid system, a circuit board of receptors for cannabinoids (yes! Our body has an entire biological system specifically created to receive the benefits from the cannabinoids in Herb) that are as much a part of our body's architecture as our taste buds and sense of hearing. The endocannibinoid system is made up of receptors in our brain and throughout our body that can help regulate the nervous system and that may even be able to counter diseases like multiple sclerosis, glaucoma, and cancer. THC, you know, that stuff in Herb that gets you high, is one type of cannabinoid. CBD (cannabidiol) is another type—it's not psychoactive, so it doesn't get you high but can help with pain relief, seizures, and a whole lot of other ailments. You can tap into the CBD benefits by searching out strains that have high amounts of CBD in them—generally these strains (like Charlotte's Web, Harlequin, and Cannatonic) all have CBD amounts above 4%. CBD can even counter or lessen the effects of THC . . . so they can be good used in tandem, especially if you're using herb for medicinal reasons. You can also find CBD-only oils and tinctures without any THC at all. CBG and CBC are other kinds of cannabinoids that don't have psychotropic effects, while CBN, CBDL, and CBL are more like THC and will get you high. From sleep aid to antiseizure medication to reducer of pressure in the eyes (what a gift for anyone with glaucoma), Herb is like the most natural pain reliever on the planet. As we learn more about herb and study its potential, we will continue to harness the many benefits of cannabinoids that naturally occur in Herb.

and eating food boosted with herb-infused CannaButter or CannaOil a decidedly different experience. To unlock the transportive properties of Herb, you have to set free the THC (delta9-tetrahydrocannabinol)—it's the THC that brings you up. To activate it, the Herb needs to be decarboxylated (page 22), a long word for "heated." This can happen through oven-toasting (if using the herb as a sprinkle or salty seasoning) or by infusing it into butter or oil: The THC in Herb is lipophilic, meaning it needs fat as a carrier (for example, it would be activated if added to broth).

Typically, when people talk about the Herb they are referring to one of two kinds: *Cannabis sativa* or *Cannabis indica*. The two varieties have distinctly different properties and effects on the body, as well as slightly different chemical compositions. Generally speaking, sativa strains are known to be energizing and inspire creative thought and an uplifted attitude. It's the "higher" of the two strains and is actually the kind of Herb that my daddy smoked (see page 29). Indica, on the other hand, usually leads to a more chill and mellow vibe that's good for relaxation. Hybrids are a third category, in which growers crossbreed sativas and indicas to pull out desirable properties of each. A lot of people argue that there's really no longer such a thing as nonhybrid Herb; people have been growing on their own for so many years that pure strains are more or less nonexistent. But knowing if the Herb you buy is sativa- or indica-forward can help you determine the effect it may have on you.

Today, at many dispensaries, you can walk up to the counter and ask a budtender for a strain that meets all your needs. Do you want notes of blueberries or citrus? (Note that the terpenes really only come into play with smoking or vaping—for edibles, these delicate flavor compounds more or less get cooked off, much like the nuance of a fine extra-virgin olive oil gets cooked out if you use it in a hot pan.) Will you be using it in the day or at night? Is it for pain relief or purely recreational? Always ask how the cannabis was grown, just as you do when you buy produce at the farmers' market. You want to support growers who farm in safe and sustainable ways. Be sure that the dispensary is testing the marijuana for any biological impurities, heavy metals, or pesticides. Only put the cleanest and most pristine matter into your body—if it applies to what you buy at the grocery store, it should apply to what you buy at your dispensary, too.

HERB IN THE KITCHEN

Chances are that at some point in your life, you've been given a pot cookie, brownie, or candy without being told how much THC is in it, without knowing when it was made or who made it, without even knowing *how* it was made or the quality of ingredients used to produce it. Thankfully, the days of questionable edibles are largely behind us, and as one state after another legalizes Herb in some form or decriminalizes possession of small amounts,* home cooks who live where it's legal to buy Herb can rest easier when it comes to making THC-enhanced foods. You will always know who made it (you!), how it was made (with love), when it was made (fresh today!), and the ingredients used to make it. You can also control how much THC each serving contains, a critical factor that is too often overlooked when it comes to edibles.

I've set up this book so you can cook the recipe with or without Herb. It's really easy to leave it out if you prefer—in most cases you just substitute a spoonful or two of butter or oil for the CannaButter or CannaOil. If the recipe *tun up*, I hope you get out of it what you want—be it euphoria, healing, mellowness, or whatever! I have kept the per-serving dosages low to encourage the moderate and joyous high that my dad liked. It should be noted, however, that the Herb grown today is much stronger than the Herb Daddy smoked, and also that ingesting Herb has a longer-lasting and more profound effect than smoking it. Be conservative with the Herb, especially when you're just starting out, so you can sample a few enhanced dishes and still be on the right side of feeling *irie*.

It should be noted that the standard per-serving dose for edibles in most states is 10 milligrams (mg). However, you will find that all of the edibles recipes in this book were developed to provide a more restrained dose of 5 mg of THC per serving based on Herb with a potency of 15% THC. This way, you can include two or even three cannabis-enhanced dishes on your table and if each person enjoys one serving of each, they will get a total of approximately 15 mg THC over the course of the evening for a completely manageable high. (And you can always double or triple the amount of CannaButter or CannaOil called for to intensify the dosage of whatever you're making.)

---

* As of this printing, 27 states plus the District of Columbia have legalized some forms of medical marijuana with Alaska, California, Colorado, Maine, Massachusetts, Nevada, Oregon, Washington, and the District of Columbia having legalized it for recreational use.

If you choose to enhance a recipe with CannaButter (page 26), CannaOil (page 25), a CannaSpice Blend (page 42), or CannaVanilla Extract (page 29), I recommend following the chart on page 25 to determine how much THC will be in each serving based on the potency of your Herb.

Of course, how the body processes THC varies from person to person. Your age, weight, metabolism, gender, level of fitness, and tolerance for THC all will affect how

SUGAR TRIM: ARE THE SAVINGS WORTH IT?

On a plant, the buds and flowers are the main source of trichomes: a sticky, oily substance that crystallizes when dried and that contains the highest concentration of cannabinoids (such as THC and CBD, among many others) and are the most valuable parts of the plant. They are generally dried and then ground to either smoke, vape, or use in edibles. Before the buds and flowers are harvested, the leaf tips directly off the bud are usually trimmed away. These leaves are coated with trichomes too, and although it's a smaller *quantity*, the *quality* of the cannabinoids in the leaves is equal to that of the buds. Because of their sugary appearance, the leaves are often called "sugar trim" while the trichomes are called "kief" (pronounced "keef"); when you apply pressure and heat to kief, you get hash.

Sugar trim can be purchased at a significantly lower cost than bud and flower, and for making edibles, this might be an attractive proposition (note that leaves from farther down on the plant usually don't have any trichomes on them). Use it to make CannaOil, CannaButter, or CannaSpice just as you would use bud and flower, then gauge whether or not you need to add more volume to achieve the same psychotropic effect. Note that this may also affect the taste of the oil or butter, making it stronger and greener in color. Additionally, if you buy sugar trim from dispensaries and invest in a three-piece multi-chamber Herb grinder (available in dispensaries and head shops), you can capture the trichomes that separate from the leaves in the bottom tier of the grinder and use it as a finishing sprinkle to both food and drinks.

your body digests and processes it. The amount of food you already have in your belly prior to eating the enhanced food will also affect your high. So it's really smart to be cautious rather than overindulge, get too high, and have a less than optimal experience.

Through experimentation and familiarity, you'll soon learn your preferences and tolerance levels. When all is said and done, eating an Herb-enhanced salad or banana fritter or cookie should leave you feeling as relaxed and happy as a glass of wine might. The difference is that the edibles take anywhere from thirty minutes to two hours to have an effect on the body and mind, so go slow, give it time to work its magic, and treat your body kindly.

DECARBOXYLATED HERB

Herb includes the compound THCA—to make the Herb psychoactive, you need to lose the CO_2 molecule (the "A") to turn it into THC. This happens when THCA is exposed to heat, as when making CannaButter and CannaOil. But for making dry spice blends (page 42) and infusions like the vanilla extract (page 29), you need to decarboxylate the cannabis first. To do this grind the buds using a multi-chamber hand grinder (¼ ounce or 7 grams if making the CannaButter, page 26, or CannaOil, page 25) and toast them in the oven at 250°F for 15 to 20 minutes, stirring every 5 minutes or so (there are as many ways to decarb Herb as there are to crack a nut but this is the method I found to work best). When it's done, the Herb will darken in color slightly and become a toasty, golden brown. Remove from the oven and cool completely before proceeding with one of the following recipes (store the decarbed Herb in an airtight and light-safe container and use it sooner rather than later). You can also decarb kief (powdery trichomes, see page 64). Just place the kief in a ramekin and proceed as described above.

TOOLS AND EQUIPMENT YOU'LL NEED FOR COOKING WITH HERB

Once you've made a supply of your favorite canna booster, be it oil, butter, or a seasoning or flavoring blend, you're all set. Simply cook the recipes as written, adding the boosted fat or flavoring as directed. To make the canna booster, however, there are a few readily available kitchen tools you will want to have on hand and if you don't own a grinder, you will need to buy one. A grinder is essential for breaking up the dried Herb to a nice, even consistency.

Herb users today have so many options when it comes to grinding their Herb for decarbing or smoking. Back in Daddy's day, you broke up dried Herb with your fingers, scissors, or a knife! Now there are sophisticated one-, two-, and three-chambered grinders that conveniently grind the Herb without it sticking to your fingers. For decarbing, uniformly ground Herb will dry more evenly. There are entire websites devoted to the pros and cons of various grinders, but my advice is this: buy something of quality that gives you pleasure and gets the job done right. Don't use a spice or coffee grinder—it will grind the Herb too powder-fine!

Grinders run from less than $20 to more than $100. Generally speaking, you're paying for the intricacy of the design and the number of parts and special features. For example, a one-piece grinder has only one chamber. It's simple, yes, but may lead to an inconsistent grind, and it can also can be difficult to dig all of the ground Herb (which gets sticky from trichomes) out from between the teeth. A two-chamber grinder allows Herb from the top chamber to fall through holes to a second chamber. So only Herb that is of a certain size falls through to the second chamber for a finer grind—the second chamber is flat, so it's easy to collect the ground Herb. The drawback is that there is no screen to collect pollen (kief), and if you go through a lot of Herb, why not collect the kief for sprinkling onto morning porridge or turning into hash? A three-chamber grinder features a screen between the second and third chambers on which the pollen accumulates.

Herb grinders can be made from wood, acrylic, aluminum, or titanium-coated aluminum. The latter two materials tend to last the longest—the teeth are less likely to break off and these grinders are just sturdier overall. However, wood is aesthetically and ergonomically pleasing to hold and use . . . the Marley Natural grinder is a three-chamber, four-piece grinder (with a screen for collecting pollen, aka kief) that blends the beauty of a wood casing with heavy-duty aluminum interior mechanisms, so you get the best of all worlds. Stay away from acrylic grinders; they are not a quality product. You're better off using a knife!

Aside from this one essential tool, you will also need an instant-read thermometer, cheesecloth, sieve or strainer, and an airtight container for storage. See page 26 if you would prefer to make your CannaOil in a slow cooker.

CANNABUTTER OR CANNAOIL can both be madeon the stovetop or in a slow cooker—the stovetop will yield a faster infusion but both CannaOil and CannaButter need to be watched closely to ensure that the temperature does not go over 250°F, as that can diminish the potency of THC. If making CannaButter, know that you need to chill the butter overnight before using, so make sure to work that timing into your cooking plan; if you're using the slow cooker method, it may take as long as 2 days before your CannaButter is ready to use, since it takes a minimum of 8 hours to infuse the butter and then an overnight chill in the fridge to separate the medicinal solids from the water by-product.

CANNAOIL

IIIIIIIIIIIIIIIIIIIIIIIIIII MAKES 2 CUPS (1 SERVING = ½ TEASPOON = 5 MG THC) IIIIIIIIIIIIIIIIIIIIIIIIIII

2 cups coconut oil, extra-virgin olive oil, or grapeseed oil

¼ ounce (7 g) cannabis flower (dose based on 15% THC herb)

1. Grind the herb using a hand grinder (you don't want it to be powder fine—think dried oregano).

2. Combine the oil and herb in a medium saucepan and bring to a low simmer over medium heat (the oil should be hot but not boiling).

3. Reduce the heat to low and cook the infusion very slowly, stirring occasionally and maintaining a temperature of between 200° and 250°F, until the top layer in the saucepan changes from watery to glossy and thick, about 2 hours.

4. Set a sieve over a medium bowl and line the sieve with cheesecloth. Pour the infusion into the sieve and let it sit until all of the oil is filtered, about 5 minutes. Fold the ends of the cheesecloth over the herb and use a rubber spatula to press on the solids, extracting as much oil as possible (discard the solids). Transfer to a jar, seal, and store at room temperature for up to 3 months. Note that CannaOil made with coconut oil will solidify; reheat gently to liquefy if necessary.

CANNABUTTER

IIIIIIIIIIIIIIIIIIIIIIIII **MAKES 1½ CUPS (1 SERVING = ½ TEASPOON = 5 MG THC)** IIIIIIIIIIIIIIIIIIIIIIIIIIIII

¼ ounce (7 g) cannabis flowers
(dose based on 15% THC herb)

4 sticks (1 pound) unsalted butter

1. Grind the herb using a hand grinder (you don't want it to be powder fine—think dried oregano).

2. Combine the butter and 2 cups water in a medium saucepan. Bring to a low simmer over medium heat. Once the butter begins to melt, add the ground cannabis.

3. Reduce the heat to low and cook the butter very gently, stirring occasionally and maintaining a temperature of between 200° and 250°F, until the top layer in the saucepan changes from watery to glossy and thick, 2 to 3 hours—you may need to add water if the temperature gets close to the 250°F mark (so the butter doesn't scorch).

4. Set a sieve over a medium bowl (preferably glass) and line the sieve with cheesecloth. Pour the infusion into the sieve and let it sit until all of the butter has been filtered, about 5 minutes. Wrap the edges of the cheesecloth over the herb and use a rubber spatula to press on the solids to extract all of the butter (discard the solids). Cover the bowl tightly and refrigerate the strained butter for at least 3 hours or overnight.

5. The next day, lift out the solid block of butter and discard any liquid remaining in the bowl. Use a paper towel to pat the surface of the butter on all sides to absorb any droplets of moisture. Wrap the butter in two layers of plastic wrap and store it in an airtight container in the refrigerator for up to 2 months or in the freezer for up to 6 months.

SLOW COOKER METHOD FOR CANNABUTTER OR CANNAOIL

1. Grind the herb using a hand grinder (you don't want it to be powder fine—think dried oregano).

2. Add the melted butter or oil to a slow cooker. If using butter, add 2 cups of hot water (some people choose not to add the water if using the slow cooker method since the

(recipe continues)

chance of scalding is very small; however, as a precaution, use water the first time and as you get to be a butter-making expert, adjust your method to suit your needs). Turn the heat to the low setting and add the ground Herb. Cover the cooker. The infusion is finished when the top layer changes from watery to glossy and thick, 8 to 24 hours (the length of cooking time depends partially on the Herb that you're using; know that cooking for a longer time won't hurt the butter, just in case you need to leave the slow cooker on overnight or while you're at work).

3. Set a sieve over a medium bowl and line the sieve with cheesecloth. Pour the infusion into the sieve and let it sit until all of the butter or oil is filtered, about 5 minutes. Wrap the ends of the cheesecloth over the Herb and use a rubber spatula to press on the solids to extract all of the liquid (discard the solids). CannaOil can now be transferred to a jar and stored at room temperature for up to 3 months. For CannaButter, cover the bowl tightly, and refrigerate the strained butter for at least 3 hours or overnight.

4. The next day, lift out the solid block of butter and discard any liquid remaining in the bowl. Pat the solid butter block with a paper towel, then wrap the butter in two layers of plastic wrap and store it in an airtight container in the refrigerator for up to 2 months or in the freezer for up to 6 months.

CANNAVANILLA EXTRACT

½ ounce (14 g) ground cannabis flower
(dose based on 15% THC herb)

6 vanilla beans

1 cup 70- to 80-proof flavorless alcohol
(such as vodka)

Decarboxylate the herb (see page 22) and cool completely. Add it to a 1-pint glass jar. Use a paring knife to split the vanilla beans lengthwise, then use the edge of the knife to scrape out the seeds. Add both the seeds and the pods to the jar. Cover with the alcohol and set aside for 4 weeks. Strain out the herb (you can remove the vanilla pods or leave them in). Transfer to a clean bottle, label, and store in a cool, dark, dry spot for up to 1 year.

DADDY'S HERB

Think of a summer-sweet heirloom tomato varietal just picked in the garden at its peak ripeness. That tomato was grown in the open air and under the hot sun and not genetically tinkered with by scientists. It probably offers more flavor than, say, a grocery store tomato in the dead of winter, right? Herb is the same. Jamaican Lambsbread is the sativa strain my father smoked. In the world of Herb, Lambsbread is considered an heirloom strain referred to as a landrace (if you smoked Herb in the 1960s or 1970s, you were likely smoking a landrace such as Lambsbread or Hindu Kush from Afghanistan or Pakistan or Acapulco Gold from Mexico). These days, growers crossbreed or hybridize strains of Herb to make cannabis that produces a very specific outcome (say superhigh THC, a pronounced pineapple flavor, or high CBD/low THC Herb used for medicinal purposes), usually using landraces as the parent strains. Like most sativa strains, Lambsbread is known for offering an uplifting high that stimulates creativity. It's difficult to find in the United States but I hope one day we find a great source for it so Marley Natural can offer the world the same kind of Herb my father liked.

DOSAGE NOTE

The recipes in this book were created to offer a very conservative/beginner concentration of 5 milligrams (mg) THC per serving based on flowers and buds from a strain with 15% THC (see the chart on page 31 for how to adjust your concentrations based on how much THC your cannabis contains). A moderate concentration would be 10 mg THC per serving (so if a recipe calls for ½ teaspoon CannaButter or CannaOil at 5 mg THC per serving, you would increase it to 1 teaspoon for 10 mg THC per serving). A high concentration would be 15 mg THC per serving (1½ teaspoons CannaButter or CannaOil at 5 mg THC per ½ teaspoon). Again, I recommend you start conservatively—you can always increase the concentration in the next batch, but nothing can take away the memory of a too-intense high! If using sugar trim (see page 21), you may consider increasing the amount of dry matter added to the butter or oil since trim may have fewer trichomes, the sticky substance where THC and other cannabinoids are concentrated.

DISCLAIMER

There are many factors to take into consideration when making CannaButter and CannaOil. The rate of absorption of THC carried by the butter or oil (or spice blend) depends on your body mass, your metabolism, fitness level, what you ate earlier in the day, your tolerance to herb, your age and gender, not to mention the cannabis strain used and how that strain was grown. Because of all of these variables, it is nearly impossible to predict the strength of the CannaButter and CannaOil that you make. The recipes on pages 25 and 26 provide a very educated guess as to how much THC each serving will yield if you begin with a 15% THC strain. The amounts of cannabis suggested in the recipes are guidelines only and should be treated as such. Because edibles are absorbed differently in the body when ingested rather than inhaled, it may take thirty minutes to two hours for the results to be felt; once the THC is active in your body, the high can last for eight hours or even longer, which is why it's best not to plan any significant activities within twelve hours of ingesting edibles, just to be safe. Begin with one serving of edibles before deciding if you want a more vivid experience.

CALCULATE YOUR DOSE

Refer to the chart below for guidelines on how much THC will be in 1 tablespoon, 1 teaspoon, or ½ teaspoon of herb-infused oil or butter, based on how much THC is in the Herb. If you want a stronger infusion, double the amount added to the fat from 0.25 ounce to 0.5 ounce (or just double the amount of infused oil or butter called for in a recipe). However, if you are planning to make more than one dish infused with Herb, stick with the lower dosage.

KEY TO DOSAGES

• **5 MG/SERVING**: a very conservative dose. Good for beginners, or if you would like to make multiple Herb-enhanced recipes to serve at a party

• **10MG/SERVING**: the average dose that most commercially available edibles target

• **15 MG/SERVING**: the higher-end average dose for commercially available edibles. This is a moderate to strong dose that can affect people differently depending on their body and tolerance levels.

• **20MG/SERVING**: a strong dose of THC. This should only be offered to experienced users.

HERB	2 CUPS BUTTER/OIL	1 TBSP OIL/BUTTER	1 TBSP OIL/BUTTER	½ TBSP OIL/BUTTER
10% THC	.25 ounce (7g)	21.8 mg	7.3 mg	3.6 mg
15%THC	.25 ounce (7g)	32.8 mg	10.9 mg	5.4 mg
20%THC	.25 ounce (7g)	43.8 mg	14.5 mg	7.3 mg
25%THC	.25 ounce (7g)	54.7 mg	18.2 mg	9.1 mg

Based on 0.25 ounce (7 grams) of Herb infused in 2 cups melted butter or oil

DIY HERB DOSAGE CALCULATION

Starting with 7 grams (7,000 mg) of 15% THC Herb, multiply as follows:

	Herb weight	×	% THC in Herb	÷	32 (2 cups = 32 TBSP)	÷	3 (1 TBSP = 3 tsp)	÷	2 (1 tsp = two x ½ tsp)	=	mg THC per ½ teaspoon serving
example	7,000 mg	×	.15	÷	32	÷	3	÷	2	=	5.4 mg

COOKING
THE MARLEY WAY

THE KITCHEN IS DEFINITELY THE MOST POPULAR PLACE TO HANG OUT at the Marley house. There you'll find music, family, laughter, conversation, and of course lots of delicious, fresh, and pure food being chopped up to go into a salad or pot or simmering away on the stovetop. Life is one giant celebration, right? And we are great at finding any reason, big or small, to gather friends and family for a good party. Some parties, though, well, they are for adults only! So put the kids to bed or send them to a friend's house because it's grown-up time. When I want to let loose and just have some fun, I'll enhance a dish (or three!) with some Herb—just enough to get our spirits high and bright, not enough to put us all into a trance . . . what fun would it be if we were all just asleep on the sofa? Whether I'm cooking "clean" or with a kick, my food often has an island beat to it because those are the flavors I grew up with and that I crave.

Jamaican culture—from food to music—is alive. It is bright and fresh and bursting with spice and a feel-good positive attitude. Anytime you put a Jamaican dish on the table it's like a party already, so when you add an Herb enhancement to the recipe, it kicks up the decibels that much more. Using Herb—whether you smoke it, vape it, or eat it—is, to me, just another part of eating clean and good. Herb is natural—it's a plant from the ground that is as pure as a bunch of thyme or parsley. While edibles are fun, they also are really so much better for you than drinking a cocktail, which can be loaded with all kinds of who-knows-what ingredients. Herb doesn't impact your liver and it's not loaded with calories or sugar, so as far as intoxicants go, it's a nice and natural ingredient you can actually feel really good about putting into your body. In this book, I'll teach you how to control how much you add to a dish so you can control your high as easily as choosing whether you'll have one glass of wine or two.

My kitchen is casual. Check your ego at the door! Here is a place to be free and happy and just let go. You'll often find people gathered around the cooktop eating some seasoned rice straight from the pot or ripping off the crispy edges of a lasagna before it has a chance to hit the table. I love entertaining—from big gatherings on weekends to cozy dinners with my closest friends. This cookbook truly reflects the way I eat—an eclectic and mostly vegetarian mix of vegetables and grains that's as good for your body as they are for your spirit and soul. My daddy chose to live his life in peace, happiness, and in unity with others. We ate a lot of fish and vegetables at home, though sometimes when at a friend's house I'd eat what they were serving—maybe curry goat, curry shrimp, brown stew chicken, oxtail with butter beans—I threw down when I got out of the house (forgive me, Mom and Dad, but confession is good for the soul).

Since I was eighteen, I've eaten a mostly vegetarian diet. In part I was inspired by my grandmother and namesake, Cedella, who was rarely sick and always just glowed and was radiant. I definitely feel the difference in my spirit and energy when I fill my diet with as many organic fruits and vegetables as I can and if using dairy products and eggs, I always buy organic, antibiotic-free, and cage-free. I know a vegetarian diet is not for everyone, though, so the recipes in this cookbook reflect that philosophy. You'll find a few recipes here and there calling for saltfish, fried fish, or pan-cooked escovitch-style fish as well as jerk chicken (always use humanely raised and preferably organic, please!).

My parents believed in whole and natural foods—Dad was drinking green juice decades before it was available in just about every grocery store! We ate very little sugar and did lots of cleanses and drank tonics to clean our blood and our insides. They believed in eating for health, and we always ate lots of nutritious home-cooked meals, many that came from our own garden. Mom loved going outside and picking fresh mint for Daddy's morning tea. For Saturday dinner, she'd whip up her Ital stews (Ital deriving its name from the word "vital," with the letter "I" being front and center to symbolize the connection to nature and to one's self, with the goal of eating as cleanly as possible to increase your life energy). On Sundays, the family would gather for dinner around

two o'clock. This was our time together, our moment to enjoy laughter and music and a little "reasoning" with Daddy and Mommy. I'm sure, when it was time to chill with friends, my parents probably experimented with adding Herb to food. Forty years ago, they most likely did what everyone else did and chopped some bud up and added it straight to a curry or stew. I think Daddy would be excited to see the evolution of how people cook with Herb now, how far cooking with herb has come (and how delicious it can be!), and how much fun and enjoyment people get when they experience an Herb-spiked dish. I'm really excited to share these family recipes with you and finally to have the opportunity to publicly marry them with Herb.

THE JAMAICAN PANTRY

Jamaican cuisine draws on influences from around the globe. British, Spanish, African, Indian, and Chinese flavors and cooking styles have all impacted our food and culture. The ingredients aren't too exotic—I'm talking thyme and coconut, cashews and Scotch bonnets, peppers and plantains, and ginger and curry.

My cooking is always fresh and good, vegetable-forward, and (for the most part) organic and healthy. I am crazy for Jamaica's national dishes like ackee (our national fruit) and saltfish, roast breadfruit, fried dumplings, rice and peas, stews and escovitch fish, but I also love lasagna, homemade guacamole, and hummus—not necessarily Jamaican but oh man, so good! Of course we all splurge every once in a while . . . who could live without the richness of extra-cheesy macaroni and cheese in their lives or brownies so fudgy they stick to your teeth! But even when I'm cooking something "American" like macaroni and cheese, it usually includes a taste of my island upbringing—from allspice to pumpkin or dried sorrel. Here is an idea of some of the ingredients that you'll find in my cupboards and in my recipes.

ACKEE: This is a fruit that grows on trees in Jamaica. Only the yellow portion is edible—the black seed is poisonous (as is the yellow fruit if the ackee is underripe!). When cooked, ackee (AH-key) has a look and texture similar to scrambled eggs, even though it has a sweet and fruity flavor. Ackee is available in cans, but I only like it fresh—ackee plus codfish is not only a delicious breakfast dish but the national dish of Jamaica.

ALLSPICE (PIMENTO): The dried berries look like peppercorns but taste like a happy combination of cloves and nutmeg. Allspice berries and ground allspice are used in a lot of traditional foods, and are essential to jerk seasoning and paste (perhaps this is why some call allspice Jamaica pepper). The tree and leaves are used to make pimento wood (which comes in the shape of logs or wood chips) and dried pimento leaves. Both add that exquisite taste to jerk chicken cooked outside on the grill . . . yeah Jamaican style.

ANNATTO: Seeds from the achiote tree, annatto is what's used to give cheddar cheese its orange color. The seeds are bloomed in hot oil and then discarded; the infused oil offers up an earthy taste and orange color to whatever you add to the pot next.

CALABAZA PUMPKIN: A large pumpkin with a velvety texture and a nice rich flavor, calabaza is similar to dense squashes like kuri and Hubbard varieties rather than more watery types like butternut. If you can't find calabaza, you can substitute yam or acorn squash.

CALLALOO: This leafy green (a variety of amaranth) is a staple in Jamaican cooking and is used as a side dish and as a stuffing for dumplings. You can find fresh callaloo at most Caribbean markets. I'd rather substitute spinach leaves or amaranth leaves (available in some farmers' markets) than use canned callaloo if I can't get the fresh leaves.

COCONUT MILK: Coconut milk is a big source of flavor in Jamaican curries, soups, and sweets. Coconut milk is made by pureeing the meat of brown coconuts with a bit of water. You can buy it canned for convenience, but really nothing beats the fresh, rich flavor of fresh coconut milk (see page 75).

COCONUT OIL: Cold-pressed coconut oil is made by extracting the oil from the coconut meat without using heat or chemicals; as a result, the oil retains its antioxidant properties and phytonutrients. Unrefined coconut oil typically has a fuller, more coconut-y flavor than refined coconut oil; however, it also has a lower smoke point (350°F versus 450°F for refined coconut oil). Refined coconut oil is bleached and deodorized, and chemicals are sometimes used to extract more oil from the meat. It's also not uncommon for refined coconut oil to be partially hydrogenated, meaning it will contain trans-fats. For all of these reasons I strongly recommend you use only unrefined coconut oil.

CURRY POWDER: Introduced to the islands by the English through colonization, Jamaicans have made curry powder their own by curbing the strong flavor (often from fenugreek) with more turmeric. If you can't find Jamaican curry, Indian curry powder can be used instead—maybe add an extra pinch of turmeric to soften its taste.

GINGER: From ginger beer to curries and Sorrel Punch (page 88), we Jamaicans love our fresh ginger. Use the edge of a teaspoon to scrape away the thin skin before finely chopping the ginger or grating it using a ginger grater or a Microplane-style rasp. Young ginger tends to be more tender and less fibrous than mature ginger.

GREEN BANANAS AND PLANTAINS: Green bananas are simply unripe bananas. They will be starchier, drier, and have less sugar than a ripe, sweet banana and you may need the help of a paring knife to peel away the skin. Plantains are even starchier and denser than green bananas and are sold in varying stages of ripeness from green to yellow and even black. The green ones are used for making tostones or can be simply boiled and served with a stew or Curry Rundown (page 73) as a potato replacement. Yellow and black (extra-ripe) plantains are used for making sweet and sticky *maduros* (fried banana slices).

GROUND PROVISIONS (ROOT VEGETABLES AND POTATOES): We do love our hearty potatoes, yams, and other ground provisions in the Caribbean. Yuca (also called cassava, manioc, or, when dried and ground, tapioca flour) looks like a long sweet potato with a bark-like skin. It's fantastic baked like steak fries. Yellow yams are quite popular in Jamaica and throughout the Caribbean—you can find them in Caribbean markets. They are larger and wider than yuca, also with a bark-like skin, though, unlike yuca, they are sold un-waxed. When handling yellow yam, wear gloves or hold the yam with a towel to steady it on the cutting board as you peel or slice (the compounds in the juice of the yam will make your hands itch!). Yellow yam cooks up with a nice, dry texture—like a sweeter version of a russet (baking) potato. Jamaican sweet potatoes are also different from the sweet potatoes you find in the U.S. First, they're not as sweet! Second, they are white fleshed with a red skin. If you don't have a Caribbean market nearby, you can try substituting Jamaican sweet potatoes with *batatas* found in Latin and some Asian markets. It's not exactly the same, but it comes closer than American sweet potatoes.

GUAVA: The size of a medium lime, guava is a wonderfully fragrant fruit. It can be used fresh in drinks or can be turned into a preserve, jelly, or paste. You can find guava paste in specialty food stores, usually in the cheese area. If you're in a Caribbean market, it'll be with the jams and such. Spanish quince paste, called *membrillo,* is a good substitute if you just can't find guava paste.

HEMP SEED: See p. 79.

PASSION FRUIT: Small and wrinkly with maroon and yellow mottled skin,

passion fruit is not a looker but, oh man, does it taste delicious. Fresh passion fruit is quite tart and while it smells beyond heavenly, it packs a sour punch. You can buy it fresh in many grocery stores (slice it in half and scoop/squeeze the pulp out into a fine-mesh sieve then use the back of a spoon to press it through) or look in the freezer section for passion fruit puree. In a pinch, you can use passion fruit juice or even melt passion fruit popsicles and just reduce the amount of sugar called for in your recipe.

PIGEON PEAS: Rice 'n peas, where would we be without you? The peas I speak of are pigeon peas, also called "gungo" peas, a dried bean that, when cooked, has a wonderfully mild flavor and smooth texture. Like all dried beans, the peas need to be soaked overnight before cooking. They're also sometimes labeled gandules in Latin markets.

SALTFISH: With so much fresh fish in the sea, why do we Jamaicans eat so much saltfish? Well way back when, cod fillets preserved in salt (like Portuguese bacalao) were traded to sugar plantation owners in exchange for Jamaican rum and molasses as a cheap protein source for the plantation's slaves. Eating salt-preserved fish became the norm and a key ingredient to many of our dishes, from ackee and saltfish to saltfish cakes and one-pots (page 176). Cod is the most common saltfish, but pollack and hake can also be salted and dried.

SCOTCH BONNET PEPPER: According to legend these incendiary chiles are so-called because they resemble a Scottish person's hat. In food terms they look like habaneros but have a sweeter flavor (though they're still plenty spicy). You can use them chopped or poke a few holes in one and drop it into a soup or stew for a slow-going roll of heat. Like all chile peppers, a lot of the heat comes from the seeds, so remove them for a milder dish and, for goodness sake, wash your hands and keep them out of your eyes!

SUGAR: I like to cook with coarse cane sugar in my food. Sugarcane is a renewable resource that can grow back after being cut down, while sugar beets, the source of much granulated sugar, have to be replanted every year. Cane sugar is also minimally processed and has a toasty flavor. We also use honey, demerara (or turbinado; essentially like sugar in the raw), regular brown sugar, and occasionally molasses in our cooking.

TALK THE TALK

In Jamaica we use some slang you may have never heard before . . . so *tun up* now and give your conversations a real island feel.

IRIE: feeling good and nice, to be cool and at peace

TUN UP: turn it up, make it exciting

BLESS UP: have a nice day

LIKKLE MORE: See you later

WAH GWAAN: what's up

PREE: checkout

ITAL: short for "vital" (see page 34)

BRUK OUT: to misbehave and get legit crazy

SOON COME: patience—it will come

BIG UP: respect

FULL JOY: happiness

RAYRAY: disorder

A SUH MI DUH MI TING: this is how I do my thing

RECIPES FOR SPICES AND SEASONINGS

We Jamaicans love our food with lots of seasoning, spices, herbs, and kick and many of the recipes in this book call for the spice blends that follow. In order to avoid giving your dishes a double dose of Herb, we have called for plain, unspiked blends when they are used to season recipes. If, however, you plan to use the blends to give a boost to unenhanced recipes, prepared foods, or snacks, just decarb some Herb (page 22) and add it to the spice blend as explained on pages 45 to 49. It's a simple and fast way to immediately turn any plain dish into a plate ready for a party. Use it as a finishing sprinkle over roasted vegetables or grilled fish, or add it to a salad dressing or plain rice, stir it into a dip, or stash it in a glass jar to give away to a friend for a thoughtful and delicious gift. Enhanced spice blends also make great giveaways—I mean anyone can bring flowers or a bottle of wine as a hostess gift but herb-enhanced jerk spice? Now you're talking (and be prepared to get invited to lots more dinner parties)!

A little bit of this and a little bit of that; making your own spice blends is really simple once you have all of the right spices on hand. Homemade blends are always so much more fresh and vibrant tasting than the pre-blended spice mixes you buy in the store. Store your spices and seasonings in a cool, dark, dry spot so they stay fresh. Un-enhanced blends stay at peak flavor for up to six months, but once you add Herb, try to use it within a month as the potency diminishes over time. Whole spices, such as whole cardamom, nutmeg, and cinnamon, can keep for up to one year, but once they're ground they are at their best within six months. Here are a few of the blends I like to have on hand.

"The divine law of giving and receiving is as natural as gravity. We shouldn't question why our feet stay firmly planted on the ground. We should simply trust in gravity because we know it works. The same holds true concerning giving and receiving. It is in giving that we receive. Our lives are open to the flow of divine blessings, and in that flow, we can give even more."

IS THERE ANYTHING more closely associated with Jamaican cooking than jerk seasoning? Naturally, it's excellent rubbed into chicken (page 141) or fish, but you can also get creative and use it for a bit of heat (and Herb!) in an unexpected place, like caramel corn (page 102).

JERK SEASONING

MAKES ABOUT ½ CUP

1½ tablespoons garlic powder

1 tablespoon onion powder

1½ tablespoons fine sea salt

1 tablespoon cane sugar

1 tablespoon dried thyme

2 teaspoons ground allspice

2 teaspoons sweet paprika

1 teaspoon freshly ground black pepper

1 teaspoon cayenne pepper

½ teaspoon ground cloves

½ teaspoon ground ginger

½ teaspoon freshly grated nutmeg

¼ teaspoon ground cinnamon

¼ teaspoon ground cumin

Combine the garlic powder, onion powder, salt, sugar, thyme, and all the spices in a bowl and stir until well blended. Transfer to a glass jar. Store in a cool, dark, dry spot for up to 6 months.

CANNABOOST: SPIKED JERK SEASONING

Decarboxylate ⅛ ounce (3.5 g) ground cannabis flower (see page 22) and cool completely. Stir into the Jerk Seasoning and mix well; ⅛ teaspoon of the spiked spice blend will deliver a 5 mg dose of THC based on 15% THC herb. To use, shake well to redistribute the cannabis and spices, then sprinkle ⅛ teaspoon over each serving. The spiked blend can be stored for up to 1 month before it will begin to lose potency.

JERK PASTE OFFERS A MARINADE-STYLE INFUSION with the same Herbaceous zip as jerk seasoning. I use it for grilling vegetables (page 123) and to season crumbly tofu for tacos (page 164) but you'll want to use it on everything from chicken for the grill to fish and meats. Soy sauce gives the paste a deep umami-quality (you know, the fifth sense of taste) that brings all the flavors together. If you decide to enhance the paste, make sure you have some CannaOil ready to go to add to the final mixture.

JERK PASTE

MAKES ABOUT ½ CUP

4 large garlic cloves, coarsely chopped

4 scallions, coarsely chopped

1 tablespoon fresh thyme leaves

1 Scotch bonnet pepper, halved (seeded for less heat)

1-inch piece fresh ginger, peeled and roughly chopped

1 tablespoon dark brown sugar

1 tablespoon coconut oil

1 teaspoon ground allspice

¼ teaspoon freshly grated nutmeg

Juice of 2 limes (about ¼ cup)

2 teaspoons soy sauce

½ teaspoon fine sea salt

1. Combine the garlic, scallions, thyme, Scotch bonnet, ginger, brown sugar, coconut oil, allspice, nutmeg, lime juice, soy sauce, and salt in a small food processor and process until smooth.

2. Scrape the jerk paste into an airtight container and refrigerate for up to 1 week.

CANNABOOST: SPIKED JERK PASTE

Substitute 2 teaspoons of CannaOil (page 25) for 2 teaspoons of the coconut oil and proceed as above. Two tablespoons of the spiked Jerk Paste will deliver a 5 mg dose of THC based on 15% THC herb.

THINK OF THIS AS A DRY BARBECUE RUB. It adds a smoky char flavor to the Guava Ketchup on page 114 and is also excellent sprinkled over roasted vegetables for a taste of the grill even when you're cooking inside.

SMOKE SALT

MAKES A HEAPING ½ CUP

2 tablespoons dried thyme

2 teaspoons ground allspice

2 teaspoons garlic powder

2 teaspoons onion powder

1½ teaspoons chipotle chile powder
  (or smoked paprika for less heat)

1 teaspoon sweet paprika

2 tablespoons coarse kosher salt

1 teaspoon coarsely ground black pepper

1. Combine the thyme, allspice, garlic powder, onion powder, chipotle chile powder, paprika, salt, and pepper in a small bowl and stir to mix well.

2. Transfer to an airtight container and store in a cool, dark, dry spot. (Note: The smoke salt blend can be stored for up to 6 months but it will lose potency the longer it sits).

CANNABOOST: SPIKED SMOKE SALT

Decarboxylate ⅛ ounce (3.5 g) ground cannabis flower (see page 22) and cool completely. Stir into the Smoke Salt; ⅛ teaspoon of spice blend will deliver a 5 mg dose of THC based on 15% THC herb. To use, shake well to redistribute the cannabis and spices, then sprinkle ⅛ teaspoon over each serving. The spiked blend can be stored for up to 1 month; after that it will begin to lose potency.

EARTHY AND HERBY with just a hint of warm sweetness from the allspice, this all-purpose herb salt is great sprinkled over pita chips (page 107) or guacamole (page 110). The sesame seeds add a little pop and crunch. Black sesame seeds look nice, too. Bring it to a party and ask your host if it's okay if you put it in a bowl on the table for guests to enjoy. If you boost it (see below), just be sure to let everyone know what to expect before they start pinchin' and stirrin'.

HERB-SESAME SALT

MAKES A HEAPING ½ CUP

3 tablespoons white or black sesame seeds

2 tablespoons dried thyme

1 tablespoon plus 1 teaspoon dried oregano

2 teaspoons ground allspice

2 tablespoons coarse kosher salt

1. Toast the sesame seeds in a small skillet over medium heat until they are golden brown, shaking the pan often, 3 to 5 minutes. Transfer to a medium plate and set aside until cooled.

2. Once the sesame seeds are cool, add them to a coffee grinder along with the thyme, oregano, and allspice. Pulse a few times to break up the seeds—you don't want a fine mixture; you want some texture. (You can also grind the ingredients using a mortar and pestle.) Add the salt and pulse 1 more time, then transfer to an airtight container and store in a cool, dark, dry spot. (Note: The spice blend can be stored for up to 6 months, but it will lose potency the longer it sits.)

CANNABOOST: SPIKED HERB-SESAME SALT

Decarboxylate ⅛ ounce (3.5 g) ground cannabis flower (see page 221) and cool completely. Stir into the spice blend; ⅛ teaspoon of spice blend will deliver a 5 mg dose of THC based on 15% THC herb. To use, shake well to redistribute the cannabis and spices, then sprinkle ⅛ teaspoon over each serving. The spiked blend can be stored up to 1 month; after that it will begin to lose potency.

THE SHAKER OF PREMADE STORE-BOUGHT GARLIC SALT is as commonplace as salt and Scotch bonnets in the Jamaican kitchen. I make my own version that is free of additives and preservatives. It provides great garlic flavor without the intense pungency of fresh garlic in dishes like Gungo Rice 'n Peas (page 185) or on fried plantain chips (page 110). Or use it to give pizza or anything with an Italian or Mediterranean flavor a lift (see CannaBoost, below) before serving.

GARLIC SALT

MAKES A HEAPING ½ CUP

¼ cup garlic powder

1½ teaspoons dried thyme

1 teaspoon dried oregano

¾ teaspoon sweet paprika

¼ cup kosher salt

Combine the garlic powder, thyme, oregano, paprika, and salt in a small bowl and stir until well blended. Transfer to an airtight container and store in a cool, dark, dry spot. Note: The Garlic Salt can be stored up to 6 months, but it will lose potency the longer it sits.

CANNABOOST: SPIKED GARLIC SALT

Decarboxylate ⅛ ounce (3.5 g) ground cannabis flower (see page 22) and cool completely. Stir into the Garlic Salt; ⅛ teaspoon of spice blend will deliver a 5 mg dose of THC based on 15% THC herb. To use, shake well to redistribute the cannabis and spices, then sprinkle ⅛ teaspoon over each serving. The spiked blend can be stored for up to 1 month; after that it will begin to lose potency.

PESTO IS a fantastic way to add an herb enhancement to nearly anything—from pasta to soup to roasted vegetables or even a sandwich. When I make it, I often use fresh basil from my garden and a combination of pine nuts and hemp seeds to give the pesto depth of flavor plus loads of amino acids, making this a protein-rich condiment. It's easy to make a double batch too and freeze half to use another time. Or add CannaOil to half the recipe and leave the rest un-enhanced for options. Hemp seeds don't contain THC so if you leave out the CannaOil, you have a very healthy and delicious pesto that won't send you on your way.

HEMP PESTO

MAKES 1¼ CUPS (5 TABLESPOONS = 5 MG THC)

2 tablespoons hulled hemp seeds, plus extra for sprinkling

¼ cup pine nuts

4 garlic cloves, roughly chopped

½ teaspoon fine sea salt

3 cups fresh basil leaves

½ cup extra-virgin olive oil

2 teaspoons CannaOil (page 25) (optional)

½ cup grated Parmigiano-Reggiano cheese

1. Combine the hemp seeds, pine nuts, garlic, and salt in a small food processor (or food processor insert) and pulverize until well combined.

2. Add the basil and pulse to chop. Then, with the machine running, drizzle in the olive oil and CannaOil (if using) and process until the mixture is well pureed. Add the Parmigiano and pulse to combine.

SERVING SUGGESTION: PESTO PASTA STUFFED VEGETABLES

With boosted pesto in your fridge it's easy to knock out a fun and colorful party dish at the drop of a hat. Toss the hemp pesto with cooked pasta (about a 1-pound box; small shapes like orzo, large pearl couscous, or ditalini work best) and use the pesto pasta to stuff vegetables. For the vegetables, grill or roast red bell peppers (halved and seeded), zucchini (halved and seeded to create a tunnel), or eggplant (halved and some of the inside scooped away to create a medium-size cup in the center of the eggplant). After they're cooked, stuff with the pesto pasta. You can stuff raw vegetables too: a halved and seeded tomato or even a seeded cucumber half. Piling the pesto pasta on top of a pitted avocado half is excellent too. Either way you'll have a completely legit dish that brings lots of color and flavor to the table.

ENHANCED DINNER PARTIES: ENTERTAINING WITH HERB

SPIKING A DISH WITH A LITTLE CANNABUTTER, CannaOil, or some CannaSpice Blend is a sure bet for making your party go from just fine to all out *irie*, and I think you'll find friends are excited to try this updated approach to Herb-enhanced cooking. But serving boosted fare comes with a responsibility to communicate clearly with your guests so they know how much of each dish they can consume without going wacky! After all, we only want positive experiences for those we invite into our homes.

In order to ensure that everyone has a great time, whether they choose to partake in Herb or not, I like to mix up enhanced foods with nonenhanced or "clean" dishes (simply leave out the Herb in the recipe and substitute an equal amount of oil, butter, spice, or vanilla)—that way, people can enjoy one serving of the enhanced dish and then one or more helpings of a "clean" dish to satisfy their appetites without overindulging. And when it comes to snacks and "can't stop with one" type foods, I just don't enhance them at all. With foods like the Jammin' Caramel-Jerk Popcorn (page 102) or Guacamole with Fried Plantain Chips (page 110), it just gets too hard to control how much people eat— they're *so* delicious that it's almost impossible *not* to eat more than one serving!

Most recipes in the book include an Herb uplift via CannaButter or CannaOil. The enhancement is moderate—usually 5 mg of THC per serving. I left the per-serving dose on the low side so guests who have never had edibles can experience a nice, mellow buzz.

On the other hand, if you're just serving one boosted dish or bringing it to a party, feel free to double or triple the amount of CannaButter or CannaOil (or other Herb-based ingredient like CannaVanilla Extract or a CannaSpice Blend) for a more standard 10 to 15 mg per serving dose. Don't forget most cannaboosters need to chill or infuse for several hours or even weeks (you can find all of those recipes on pages 25 to 29).

Of course I hope you'll love these dishes so much you'll want to serve them all the time—including situations where a cannaboost would not be appropriate. When that's the case, simply replace the Herb-enhanced oil, butter, or seasoning with the same amount of olive oil, coconut oil, butter, or spices.

If you are new to cooking with Herb, I recommend you start with one Herb-enhanced recipe and see how it goes, especially when entertaining. Once you've got the hang of cooking and entertaining with Herb-spiked food you can even serve multiple Herb-enhanced dishes at a dinner party. Since no dish will deliver more than 5 mg of THC per serving, you could potentially serve a cannabis-enhanced soup, side dish, and dessert so guests would get a total of 15 mg of THC over the course of the evening—a less conservative dose, yet one that more experienced cannabis users can happily handle. Be sure to read the "Ten Commandments (Plus a Couple Extra) of Cooking with Herb" on page 58 before you cook a recipe or have people over to enjoy.

The order in which you serve the enhanced dishes can also make a difference in your guests' overall experience. When it's ingested rather than smoked or inhaled, the THC in Herb can take thirty minutes to two hours to take effect, so it's really best to eat spiked dishes early on in an evening. That doesn't mean you can't enhance dessert with Herb! You just want to introduce a nice vibe early, maybe with an appetizer or first course and keep the feeling good through dessert rather than wait until your main course to serve the first taste of a spiked dish.

I've put together a few sample menus for when a little Herb might be a nice addition to a menu (believe me, it makes the Oscars a whole lot more interesting!). Here are some suggestions, but why not let yourself be free and come up with your own versions?

MENUS

||||||||||

TAKE IT EAZY WEEKEND BRUNCH

Smoke Ring Stuffed Bagels (PAGE 77)

Catch a Star Juice (PAGE 97; "CLEAN")

Hemp, Kale, and Apple Salad (PAGE 126)

Grilled Jerk Vegetables with Lime Vinaigrette (PAGE 123; "CLEAN")

Veggie bacon or turkey bacon

Baked and Glazed Pumpkin-Ginger Donuts (PAGE 205)

||||||||||

SPA PARTY

Marley Family Green Juice (PAGE 91)

Superpowered Hemp Dip (PAGE 101; "CLEAN") WITH LOTS OF VEGGIES FOR DIPPING

About'a Turn Mango Salad (PAGE 129)

Snapper Escovitch (PAGE 139)

Citrus-Ginger Sorbet with Raise-Up Raspberry Sauce (PAGE 194; "CLEAN")

A few spa treatments! See pages 216 to 224.

||||||||||

SUNDAY GAME DAY

Guacamole with Fried Plantain Chips (PAGE 110; "CLEAN")

Callaloo and Smoky Gouda Fried Dumplings (PAGE 104)

Jerk Tofu Taco with Black Bean–Mango Salsa (PAGE 164)

Passionate Dark and Stormy

(PASSION JUICE, PAGE 95, "CLEAN"; PLUS DARK RUM AND GINGER BEER)

Ovaltine Biscuits (PAGE 210) and vanilla ice cream

||||||||||

PICNIC LUNCH

Chips and salsa (STORE-BOUGHT)

Spicy Jamaican Patties (PAGE 147)

Spinach Salad with Goat Cheese, Pickled Beets, and Pine Nuts (PAGE 133; "CLEAN")

Island Potato Salad (PAGE 181)

Lots of fruit!

Guava Cream Cheese–Stuffed Banana Muffins (PAGE 63)

MOVIE NIGHT

Jammin' Caramel-Jerk Popcorn (PAGE 102; "CLEAN")
Babaghanouj Mashup (PAGE 113; "CLEAN") with Homemade Pita Chips (PAGE 107)
Island Beet Burgers with Avocado and Jerk-Fried Onions (PAGE 167)
Smoky Baked Yuca Wedges with Guava Ketchup (PAGE 114; "CLEAN")
Double-Chocolate Brownie Truffles (PAGE 207)

DINNER IN THE GARDEN

Chilled Sorrel Punch (PAGE 88)
Fresh Beet "Hummus" with Homemade Pita Chips (PAGE 107; "CLEAN")
Grilled Jerk Chicken with Tamarind Barbecue Sauce (PAGE 141)
Gungo Rice 'n Peas (PAGE 185; "CLEAN")
Rum Raisin and Grape-Nuts Ice Cream (PAGE 191)

A NICE TIME DINNER

Saltfish Fritters with Fiery Dippin' Sauce (PAGE 118; "CLEAN")
Pepperpot Soup (PAGE 179)
My Veg Lasagna (PAGE 152) and garlic bread
Marley Passion Cheesecake (PAGE 202)

EASY STORE-BOUGHT ADD-ONS FOR ENHANCED MENUS

It's important to have lots of nonenhanced ("clean") foods on hand
for your hungry guests so everyone is sure to get enough to eat!
Here are some ideas to keep bellies full and your friends happy.

- Cheese and crackers
- Store-bought mezze platter (hummus, stuffed grape leaves, olives, roasted peppers and pita for dipping)
- Small balls of fresh mozzarella (bocconcini) with cherry tomatoes and basil
- Chips and salsa
- Toasted bread topped with smashed avocado and flaky sea salt
- Oven-warmed cashews and peanuts (or fry in a skillet with a little oil and spices)
- Smoked salmon with cream cheese, capers, and pumpernickel bread

THE TEN COMMANDMENTS
(PLUS A COUPLE EXTRA)
OF COOKING WITH HERB

1. Edibles take thirty minutes to two hours to be fully absorbed into your body. Be patient—you can always eat a little more, but you'll have to wait many hours for the psychotropic effects of THC to chill if you ingest too much.

2. Always know how much THC your Herb has in it before making CannaButter (page 26), CannaOil (page 25), a CannaSpice Blend (page 42), or CannaVanilla Extract (page 29). If your source does not know the breakdown of the Herb, it's time to find a new one (or grow your own if your state allows it!—see page 20).

3. It's better to underdose than overdo it. My recipes are based on 15% THC Herb. Strains with a higher THC level should be used more conservatively. You can always make the next batch of CannaButter, CannaOil, CannaSpice Blend, or CannaVanilla Extract stronger (or simply use more butter or oil in the recipe) if the first time around your high is too mild.

4. Set up a comfy spot before you begin, especially if you're inviting people who have never tried Herb-enhanced food before.

5. Put on some sweet reggae music. Environment plays a huge factor in the enjoyment of your experience.

6. Be thoughtful when combining alcohol and Herb. Alcohol can compound the good *and* bad psychological effects of Herb. That said, it does take thirty minutes to two hours for the Herb to kick in, so starting the evening with a glass of wine or a cocktail is usually just fine.

7. Always label food made with Herb, including how much represents a single portion and how much THC that portion contains (you can also preportion items like popcorn into single-serving cups). If hosting an uplifted dinner party, be sure to mix non–Herb-infused dishes into your menu so everyone can feel well fed and satisfied without overindulging on the enhanced dishes.

8. Never drive after eating food infused with Herb. Ever.

9. Remember that edibles are more intense when consumed on an empty stomach.

10. Herb-enhanced food is for adults only. Ensure that children do not have easy access to Herb-infused products.

11. Have orange juice and an electrolyte beverage like Gatorade handy in case anyone overdoes it. Increasing your blood sugar level can help moderate a high. Some also say a lemon slice under the tongue helps.

12. Clear your schedule for twelve hours after you plan on eating Herb-infused food—just in case.

13. FullJoy yourself and be open to all possibilities.

I

GOOD MORNING JAH

"Misty mornin',
don't see no sun /
I know you're out there
somewhere having fun."
—"MISTY MORNING," BOB MARLEY

nhanced morning foods aren't just about "wake and bake," but about starting your day with a receptive mind and heart. My mother, Rita, likes to say that Herb is an eye-opener, and that there are many people walking around with their eyes open but they still can't see. Herb helps us to see, and what better time to open your eyes and embrace the day than in the morning? When infusing breakfast foods with Herb butter or oil, it's important to pay close attention to the strain being used. Generally speaking, uplifting sativa-forward strains are better for morning routines, especially for a productive day! Save the mellow indica-dominant strains for later in the day when you can be more chill (or maybe for those breakfast-for-dinner kinds of days!). Maybe pack some Herb-infused guava-stuffed muffins for a hike or eat herb-enhanced cornmeal porridge before setting out on a cold morning. We Marleys have always maintained that Herb helps us rise above—we don't want to be under anything; Herb can help achieve a greater "over"standing of ourselves and the world.

ENHANCED MUFFINS are a great pack-ahead and go option for a hike, a picnic, or any place where a portable spiked treat might be welcome (long train ride? all-day concert?). These have some banana for fiber and complex carbs in the form of white whole wheat flour for slow-burning energy. (For an even more nutritious muffin, use all white whole wheat flour—the muffins will be a little heartier.) They are topped with crunchy granola, but the real magic is in the gooey guava–cream cheese filling made using guava paste; it's such a tasty surprise when you bite in (see page 40 for more about guava paste). The granola topping adds extra crunch and deliciousness.

GUAVA CREAM CHEESE–STUFFED BANANA MUFFINS

MAKES 12 MUFFINS (5 MG THC PER MUFFIN)

GRANOLA TOPPING

½ cup granola

¼ cup all-purpose flour

¼ cup packed dark brown sugar

¼ teaspoon fine sea salt

3 tablespoons coconut oil

MUFFINS

2 large cage-free eggs

⅔ cup packed dark brown sugar

½ cup 2% plain Greek yogurt

2 tablespoons CannaOil (page 25; preferably made with coconut oil)

2 very ripe bananas, mashed

1 cup all-purpose flour

1 cup white whole wheat flour

2 teaspoons baking powder

1 teaspoon ground cinnamon

½ teaspoon fine sea salt

¾ cup cream cheese

¾ cup guava paste

1. **MAKE THE GRANOLA TOPPING:** Mix together the granola, flour, brown sugar, and salt in a medium bowl. Add the coconut oil and use your fingers to rub everything together.

2. **MAKE THE MUFFINS:** Preheat the oven to 350°F. Lightly coat 12 cups of a muffin tin with cooking spray or line with paper muffin liners.

(recipe continues)

3. Whisk together the eggs, brown sugar, yogurt, CannaOil, and bananas in a large bowl. Set a large sieve over the bowl and add the flours, baking powder, cinnamon, and salt. Sift the dry ingredients over the wet, then use a rubber spatula to fold the mixture together.

4. Fill each muffin cup half full with batter. Add a tablespoon of the cream cheese and top with a tablespoon of the guava paste. Sprinkle the muffins with the granola topping.

5. Bake the muffins until they resist pressure when lightly pressed, 20 to 25 minutes (a cake tester doesn't work so well in this case since the muffins are stuffed with cream cheese). Remove from the oven and cool for 10 minutes in the pan. Transfer the muffins to a wire rack to cool completely before serving.

A PINCH HERE AND THERE

Waste not want not, right? When grinding dried flower and bud, sometimes an off-white crystalline powder can fall off—this is good stuff—it's called kief, or more properly, the "trichomes." This is where the THC, CBD, and other cannabinoids are found. Invest in a multi-chamber hand grinder that has a screened catchment area at the bottom and collect the kief to sprinkle over cereal or granola, add to juice or coffee . . . or really anything. Kief is also what is used to make hash . . . but you need a *lot* of kief to do that! Saving pinches to add to a dish is a smart way to avoid wasting any precious part of the Herb. The kief does need to be decarbed to activate the THC and unlock its psychoactive properties; see page 22 for some how-to.

CINNAMON LEAVES

Cinnamon sticks and leaves from cinnamon trees tied in small bundles are often sold in outdoor food markets in Jamaica. Cinnamon leaves have a deep, somewhat spicy and musky flavor, and many old-timers believe their essential oils and phytonutrients are antibacterial and aid digestion. Add cinnamon leaves to any recipe that calls for cinnamon sticks for an extra layer of spicy, earthy flavor. They can be found dried (like bay leaves) in Caribbean markets.

THE FIRST MEAL OF THE DAY in Jamaica is often a porridge, maybe oatmeal, green banana, or one like this sweet and creamy cornmeal porridge. It's warm and hearty, and Mama used to say it's a thinking food—it fuels your brain and fills you up with energy. Sometimes I like to sprinkle wheat germ on top for extra nutrients. If you are into the practice of saving kief after grinding Herb, try sprinkling a little pinch of it (see page 64 for more on kief and trichomes) over the porridge.

JAMAICAN CORNMEAL
PORRIDGE

SERVES 4 (5 MG THC PER SERVING)

8 allspice berries

4 cinnamon leaves or 2 cinnamon sticks

¼ teaspoon ground cinnamon

¾ cup fine cornmeal

¼ teaspoon freshly grated nutmeg

¾ cup sweetened condensed milk

2 teaspoons CannaOil (optional; page 25), made with coconut oil

1 teaspoon vanilla extract

¼ teaspoon fine sea salt

¼ teaspoon almond extract

1. Combine 4 cups water, the allspice, cinnamon leaves (or cinnamon sticks), and ground cinnamon in a medium saucepan. Bring the mixture to a boil.

2. While the water and spices come to a boil, whisk together the cornmeal with ¾ cup cold water until smooth.

3. Add the cornmeal mixture to the boiling water, whisking to combine. Reduce the heat to medium-low and cook, stirring occasionally, until the mixture is thick, about 20 minutes.

4. Stir in the nutmeg, then add the condensed milk, CannaOil (if using), vanilla, salt, and the almond extract. Stir to combine and remove from the heat. Divide among 4 bowls and serve.

WHEN I WAS YOUNGER, when the bananas became too overripe and sugar-rich to eat we turned them into luscious and sweet, crispy banana fritters—what a treat! The trick to crispy edges and a deep brown sugar flavor in the fritter is to fry the bananas in butter and coarse cane sugar before adding the batter to the pan. The bananas caramelize and become sticky-good—when you flip the fritter it's like a mini upside-down cake. If you have CannaVanilla Extract (page 29) on hand, you can replace ½ teaspoon of the regular vanilla with it, and then omit the spiked butter or oil.

BANANA FRITTERS

SERVES 4 (MAKES 8 FRITTERS; 5 MG THC PER SERVING)

2 very ripe medium bananas

½ cup whole milk

1 large cage-free egg

7 tablespoons unsalted butter, melted

1 tablespoon cane sugar

1 teaspoon vanilla extract

2 teaspoons CannaButter (page 26) or CannaOil (page 25)

1½ cups all-purpose flour

½ teaspoon baking soda

½ teaspoon fine sea salt

4 tablespoons demerara or turbinado sugar

Powdered sugar (optional)

1. Peel the bananas and add one and a half of them to a large bowl, then use a fork to smash the bananas into a pulp. Whisk in the milk, egg, 3 tablespoons of melted butter, the sugar, vanilla, and CannaButter.

2. Slice the remaining ½ banana on a diagonal into eight ¼- to ½-inch-thick pieces.

3. Whisk together the flour, baking soda, and salt in a medium bowl. Add the flour mixture to the banana-milk mixture and stir to combine.

4. Add 2 tablespoons of the melted butter to a large nonstick skillet over medium heat. Add 2 tablespoons of the demerara sugar and cook, stirring slowly but constantly, until the sugar is semi-dissolved and the butter foams, about 30 seconds.

5. Add a banana slice to each quadrant of the pan. Cook 30 seconds, then flip the banana slices over and reduce the heat to medium-low.

6. Use about ⅓ cup of batter to cover each banana slice, making 4 pancakes. Cook until the bottoms are browned and the edges are starting to look set, 1½ to 2 minutes. Tilt the skillet occasionally to redistribute the butter and sugar mixture. Flip the fritters and cook the other side for 1 minute, then transfer to a plate.

7. Use tongs and a paper towel to wipe out any burnt bits of sugar, then repeat the entire process, using the remaining 2 tablespoons butter, 2 tablespoons sugar, banana slices, and fritter batter. Serve the fritters plain or sprinkled with powdered sugar.

HERB + LIFE:
EXERCISE, THE ULTIMATE HIGH

I've always had a lot of stamina, probably thanks to all the exercise I got when I was young and living in the mountains of Jamaica with my family. Every evening we'd run down the hills and then hike back up; the air was so pure and clean, it was totally exhilarating. And as a performer, you get used to expending a certain amount of energy on a daily basis. Being on stage is, in itself, its own kind of cardio workout, and when I was younger and performing in the Melody Makers, often times I'd smoke some Herb after a show to calm down and help me resettle myself after being "on" for hours and hours.

   Don't think about Herb only as something to help you recover after strong exertion, though. It can be nice to take in a little Herb before doing yoga or going on a hike or bike ride. Clearing your mind with Herb before doing bodywork can be a wonderful way to re-center yourself, focus, and look inward as you work to strengthen and tone your muscles and limbs. If you're preparing for a hike, enjoying some cannabis-enhanced food (or even a green juice) beforehand can pay off when, after you climb that hillside, you take in the natural beauty of the area in a whole new way. A sativa-forward strain is best for high-energy work; I would even recommend a sativa-dominant herb for yoga, too . . . the last thing you need is for an indica-heavy strain to cause you to fall asleep in your downward dog!

"Go ahead and get out beyond the comfortable trap of all you're used to and all you're sure of. Challenge yourself, stretch yourself, and reach beyond yourself all the way to the fulfillment of your most outstanding dreams."

YOU WANT TO FEEL GOOD? You make a rundown! This is Jamaican comfort food at its best, and since it is loaded with healthy veggies, while it will fill you up it won't weigh you down. When I'm hosting a brunch, I'll often use up all the veggie odds and ends in the fridge to make a rundown—it can easily be doubled or tripled for a big group. Any time you add coconut milk to a dish it immediately takes on a sexy vibe—and it's even sexier *tun up* with some Herb, too. Like lots of saucy Jamaican dishes, we begin by "burning" the garlic, ginger, and curry powder in some annatto oil (page 74). Burning it doesn't mean you actually burn it; you just give it a good hard cooking in the pan. The flavors of the coconut, ginger, garlic, and curry are very bold, making this recipe a great one for introducing friends who might be wary of Herb flavor to a great-tasting Herb-enhanced dish.

CURRY RUNDOWN
WITH BOILED GREEN BANANA

SERVES 4 (5 MG THC PER SERVING)

BOILED GREEN BANANA

2 green (unripe) bananas

1 teaspoon kosher salt

1 teaspoon fresh lemon or lime juice

CURRY RUNDOWN

2 tablespoons coconut oil

1 tablespoon annatto seeds

2 tablespoons Jamaican curry powder

4 medium garlic cloves, minced

½ teaspoon grated fresh ginger

4 scallions, finely chopped

1 small yellow onion, finely chopped

1 carrot, peeled and cut at an angle into ½-inch-thick slices

1 portobello mushroom, stemmed and chopped into bite-size pieces

2½ teaspoons kosher salt

1½ cups bite-size broccoli pieces

1 medium zucchini, cut at an angle into ½-inch-thick slices

½ green bell pepper, chopped into bite-size pieces

½ Scotch bonnet pepper, seeded and minced

3 cups light coconut milk

8 fresh thyme sprigs

¼ teaspoon garlic powder

3 large okra (optional), cut at an angle into ½-inch-thick slices

2 teaspoons CannaOil (page 25), preferably made with coconut oil

(recipe continues)

1. **MAKE THE BOILED GREEN BANANA:** Slice the ends off of the bananas and then halve each crosswise. Use a sharp knife to slit through the peel down the length of the banana. Place the banana halves under cold running water and remove the peels. Use the back of a knife to scrape away any tough bits of peel still sticking to the banana.

2. Bring a medium saucepan of water to a boil over high heat. Add the salt and lemon juice (this prevents the banana from browning). Add the bananas and cook until the tip of a paring knife easily slides into a banana without resistance, about 20 minutes. Remove from the heat and set the bananas (still in the water) aside.

3. **MAKE THE CURRY RUNDOWN:** Combine the coconut oil and annatto seeds in a large pot and cook over medium heat until the annatto seeds tint the oil orange, stirring often, about 2 minutes. Pour the oil through a fine-mesh sieve into a bowl (discard the seeds) and return the oil to the pot. Add the curry powder, garlic, and ginger, and cook, stirring often, until the ginger and garlic are fragrant, about 1 minute.

4. Stir in half of the scallions and all the onion and cook, stirring often, until the onion softens and starts to brown around the edges, 3 to 4 minutes. Then stir in the carrot, mushroom, and 1 teaspoon of the salt and cook until the mushrooms start to get glossy and release their water, 2 to 3 minutes. Stir in the broccoli, zucchini, bell pepper, Scotch bonnet, and ½ teaspoon of the salt and cook until the zucchini starts to soften, about 3 minutes.

5. Pour in the coconut milk. Add the thyme sprigs, garlic powder, and remaining 1 teaspoon salt and bring the liquid to a simmer over medium-high heat. Add the okra (if using) and the CannaOil. Cook until the okra are tender, 2 to 3 minutes.

6. Drain the bananas and divide them among 4 bowls. Serve the rundown over the bananas and sprinkle with the remaining scallions.

CRACKING COCONUT AND MAKING COCONUT MILK

Try using fresh coconut milk once and I swear, you'll never go back to cans! Not only is it fresh, sweet, and healthy, but it's better for the planet too—less processing, less waste, less carbon footprint, right?

TO CRACK A COCONUT: Use a meat mallet or rubber mallet to hit the coconut around its midsection, turning it in your hand until it cracks apart. Pour out and save the coconut water (to use in a recipe, to drink, or to make coconut milk—see below). Use the mallet to break apart the halves—the coconut meat should easily separate from the husk.

TO MAKE COCONUT MILK: Slice the coconut meat into 1/8-inch-thick strips and place them in a blender. Pour the reserved coconut water into a measuring cup and add enough filtered cold water to reach to the 4-cup mark. Add the water mixture to the blender with 1 cup cane sugar (optional—or add less if you want it less sweet) and process for 1 minute, until the coconut milk is well blended. Pour the milk through a fine-mesh sieve into a bowl, pressing on the solids with the back of a spoon to extract as much liquid as possible. Save the milk for up to a week in the fridge—but hey, it's not going to last that long!

TO GRATE COCONUT: Remove the coconut meat from the shell and use a vegetable peeler to remove the brown skin. Use the small holes of a box grater to grate the coconut. One coconut will yield about 1 1/3 to 1 1/2 cups of lightly packed grated coconut.

THIS IS A GOOD ONE for those times when you just want to make something impromptu spiked with Herb that's delicious, simple, and fast. It's as perfect on the brunch table as it is in a picnic basket. Lox makes a special-occasion food, so even though this cool-looking dish takes only minutes to make, it seems kind of fancy. I scoop out some of the doughy center of the bagel and stuff it with a smoked salmon spread made with cream cheese, cucumber, red onion, dill, and capers—and a little CannaOil too, which works really well with the smoky taste of the salmon. When you slice it in half, it looks like a little bit of wizardry was cast upon the bagel—it really does look "stuffed." If you don't have CannaOil to add to the cream cheese, you could sub in an Herb-enhanced spice blend (pages 45 to 50).

SMOKE RING STUFFED BAGELS

SERVES 4 (5 MG THC PER SERVING)

8 ounces cream cheese, at room temperature

1 small cucumber, grated on the medium holes of a box grater

¼ small red onion, minced

2 tablespoons finely chopped fresh chives

2 tablespoons brined capers, rinsed, drained, and coarsely chopped

2 tablespoons finely chopped fresh dill

4 ounces lox, finely chopped

Fine sea salt, if needed

2 teaspoons CannaOil (page 25)

4 bagels, split

1. Place the cream cheese in a medium bowl and stir in the cucumber, red onion, chives, capers, and dill. Once it is well combined, fold in the smoked salmon and taste, adding a pinch or two of salt if needed. Stir in the CannaOil.

2. Pull out some of the bready insides of each bagel half. Use a spoon to fill each bottom half with one-quarter of the cream cheese mixture, mounding it slightly. Replace the top bagel half and gently press together. Slice crosswise before serving.

FRIED DUMPLINGS (also known as Johnnycakes) are one of the most common breakfast "withs" you come across in Jamaica—they are the must-have side dish to the custardy fruit called ackee (which looks like scrambled eggs when sautéed). Add saltfish and you have our national dish. In Jamaica where the humidity is high and bread goes bad fast, dumplings not only taste so good but they make sense too as they can be quickly made and fried fresh. Hulled hemp seeds (see page 79 for more information) are a wonder food, a perfect protein that brings the whole spectrum of amino acids to these dumplings; but don't worry, the hemp seeds you buy in the grocery store are agricultural hemp seeds—they don't have the THC that gets you high, so no fears about double dosing.

HEMP SEED
FRIED DUMPLINGS

SERVES 4 (MAKES 8; 5 MG THC PER SERVING)

2 cups all-purpose flour

¼ cup cornmeal

¼ cup hulled hemp seeds

1 tablespoon baking powder

½ teaspoon fine sea salt

3 tablespoons cold unsalted butter,
   cut into small pieces

2 teaspoons cold CannaButter (page 26)

¼ cup milk

¼ cup ice water

Vegetable oil, for frying

Good-quality butter, for serving

Flaky sea salt, for serving

Honey, for serving

Hot sauce, for serving

1. Whisk together the flour, cornmeal, hemp seeds, baking powder, and salt in a large bowl. Add the butter and CannaButter and use your fingers to work it into the dry ingredients until the mixture looks like crumbly meal with no butter pieces larger than a small pea.

2. Drizzle in the milk and use a fork to stir it into the dry ingredients just until incorporated, then add the water. Continue to stir with a fork until the dough holds together when pressed in the palm of your hand. Knead the dough until it is mostly smooth (it will be

rough textured from the cornmeal and hemp seeds), about 3 minutes. Cover the dough with a damp paper towel and set aside for 30 minutes.

3. Divide the dough into 8 equal pieces and roll each one into a ball. Pour ½ inch of oil into a large skillet and set over medium-high heat. Once the oil shimmers, add the dumplings to the skillet, pressing them down slightly to flatten. Fry on both sides, using a spoon to baste the tops with hot oil as they cook (this helps them puff extra tall), until they're golden brown, about 5 minutes total. Transfer the dumplings to a plate lined with paper towel to cool just a minute or two before serving with butter, flaky salt, honey, and hot sauce.

HEMP FOR MOTHER EARTH

Hemp is a wondrous plant that is also easy on our environment. First, it can grow almost anywhere, in many climates and soil types (America imports hemp largely from Canada and China and I can't imagine environments more diverse than those). Second, hemp grows even faster than a weed (ever wonder where Herb got its nickname?). It doesn't need a lot of room or water—actually half as much as cotton requires—meaning farmers can grow lots of it in a small space. It also extracts toxins and pollutants from soil, and absorbs carbon dioxide. What a miracle!

Hemp can be made into paper using fewer chemicals than are needed to make paper from wood, it can be made into textiles and carpeting, concrete-type blocks, mulch, fiberglass, composites that auto manufacturers are already using in place of plastic for car parts, and it can even produce fuel. Not to mention the many, many health benefits you can realize by eating the seeds (a fiber-rich superfood that provides omega-3 and omega-6 fatty acids plus a generous assortment of nutrients, including magnesium and a host of vitamins). Hemp seed is also a perfect protein, meaning it contains all the essential amino acids our bodies need. As Herb becomes more accepted medicinally and recreationally, I hope the trend spills over to the agricultural side (right now, it's illegal for farmers to grow hemp under the provisions of the Controlled Substances Act), so farmers will finally be allowed grow hemp to heal our Mother Earth and support society in a less harmful, more sustainable way.

2

||||||||||||||||||||||||||||||||||||

ANYTIME
QUENCHERS

*"Hey Rastaman,
hey what you say,
give me some of you sense."*
—"ONE DRAW," RITA MARLEY

Drinking Herb is a really great and healing way to feel its full power and its medicinal effects. My parents used to grow Herb in their garden in Jamaica. The Herb was like a part of our family—Mommy would talk to the plants and sing to them too. She'd add ashes from our fire to the soil to supplement the natural nutrients in the garden and help the Herb grow strong and lush. When you grow your own Herb, you can use the raw leaves in teas and tisanes or even juice them like wheatgrass or add them to a smoothie for the full-on fiber-packed benefit. Since the leaves aren't being heated (or heated for long enough periods of time) the THC isn't active, so you get the healthy qualities of the plant (such as antioxidants and CBDA, the unheated version of CBD, a cannabinoid that is used medicinally without psychotropic effects) without the high (see page 18 for more information). Warm tea made with dried Herb (called *bhang* in India, where it is a traditional tonic; or just Herb tea in Jamaica) can help with all kinds of stomach ailments, aches, and cramps. Note that unlike a cold beverage, the THC in a warm beverage may be activated, especially if fat, like a teaspoon of butter or cream, is added. Fresh mint and rosemary were Mommy and Daddy's favorite accent flavors added to their Herb tea. If you're adding CannaOil to a drink, you want to pay mind to the kind of Herb used in your infusion—remember, sativa is for feeling creatively uplifted and inspired while indica is for that mellow mood.

DRINKING MINT TEA in the morning is a Jamaican tradition. It's said to stimulate the digestive system to help get the day started off right. We used to grow mint in our garden in Jamaica; I remember my parents picking it fresh and drinking it simply steeped in hot water, adding just a little honey to make our mornings (or evenings) sweet. You can also add ginger, a sprig of rosemary, or a squeeze of lemon if you like. If you have fresh herb leaves, you can add them too; the effect will be mellow since you're not steeping the leaves in the tea for hours and hours. Since the fresh leaves may be harder to come by, here I have added ½ teaspoon coconut CannaOil to the hot infusion for a more medicated mint tea. This is so nice and refreshing, and is also extra good over ice for a mellow summer afternoon.

MORNING MINT TEA

MAKES 1 SERVING (ABOUT 1 CUP; 5 MG THC PER SERVING)

½ cup packed fresh mint leaves

Boiling water

½ teaspoon CannaOil (optional; page 25), made with coconut oil

Squeeze of honey

Fill a mug with the mint leaves and pour boiling water over them. Add the CannaOil (if using; ½ teaspoon per serving) and honey, stir, and set aside for 4 minutes to steep. Leave the mint in while you drink the tea.

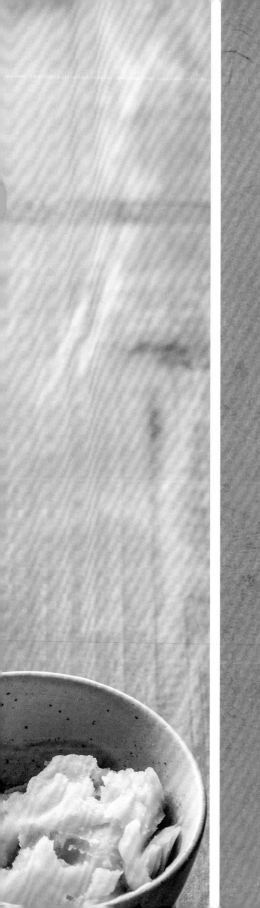

TRADITIONAL JAMAICA COCOA TEA

On Sundays at the Marley house, you'd commonly find an aunty or mommy in the kitchen making a saucepan of cocoa tea for everyone before dinner preparations began. Cocoa tea is a warm hot chocolate–like drink made from water, cinnamon leaves (page 66), nutmeg, and a compressed nugget of raw chocolate about the size of a golf ball that got grated right into the saucepan. The cocoa tea was simmered a good long while to create harmony among all the ingredients. Once the oil speckled the surface of the water, we'd pour in some coconut milk and let it simmer some more until dots rose again. Then we added a splash of vanilla and almond extract, some raw sugar, and a pinch of salt and we'd have a soothing, rich, and comforting drink to sip on that made Sundays extra sweet. If you have a Caribbean market nearby, you may be able to find cocoa balls and cinnamon leaves . . . or simply grate a nugget (about 2 ounces) of unsweetened chocolate into a small saucepan of simmering water and add $1/2$ cinnamon stick too, along with a pinch or two of freshly grated nutmeg. This is so good before bedtime—and it's extra-nice spiked with a $1/2$ teaspoon coconut CannaOil (page 25; when it's cool out, your coconut CannaOil can solidify as shown) at the end along with the vanilla and almond extracts.

HERB + LIFE:
A LITTLE THIS-N-THAT ABOUT JUICING

Drinking juices and smoothies is a great way to bring the pure nutrition of fruits and vegetables into your body, and that's true for fresh Herb leaves as well. Since the THC in fresh herb leaves isn't activated you won't get any of the "high" from the Herb. Many believe, however, that raw cannabis juice is loaded with nutrition and antioxidants that interact with the immune system and act as a modulator with the immune and nervous systems to better our health. The drawback is that you need *a lot* of leaves to get a good wheatgrass-size shot of Herb. If you grow your own, though, or have access to organically grown and healthy plants, you should give it a try. Raw Herb juice can be bitter, so it's best added to a smoothie or juice that has other sweet components like carrot, pineapple, or even a bit of honey to mellow out the intense flavor. About 1/3 to 1/2 cup of raw Herb leaves will yield approximately 1 ounce (2 tablespoons) of juice.

We don't have a fancy juicer at my house, so for us, it makes more sense to blend raw leaves with other ingredients smoothie-style the old-fashioned way—using a blender. I like thick smoothie-like juices because they deliver all of the fiber and nutrients locked in the peel and flesh of the fruit (and Herb leaves offer a lot of healthy fiber); but if you prefer pulp-free juices, simply strain the blended mixture through a fine-mesh sieve. You'll end up with about 50 percent less juice (and less fiber, too).

When juicing, add the softer fruits or vegetables, like your cucumbers, berries, or pineapple to the blender first. Then add the tougher items like carrots, leafy greens, and herbs. Lastly, add the ice cubes, any citrus juice or water. This way, the blender purees the juicy items first, creating enough of a slush to pull down the harder-to-blend ingredients. And just when your blender is ready to call out *what de rass*! it brings down the ice cubes to chill the juice and deliver more momentum to the blending.

TYPICALLY A CHRISTMAS DRINK, this punch can be served hot or cold and is a great way to get the party started. It's made with sweet/tart dried sorrel, the sepal of the hibiscus flowers that grow all over Jamaica. When steeped overnight in water, the sepals give off a gorgeous fuchsia color that never fails to bring me straight back to the Caribbean.

I like to let the sorrel have a good soak with spices and orange slices before mixing with the fruit and either CannaVanilla Extract or CannaOil depending on whether I'm serving the punch chilled or warm (for the warm punch variation, see opposite). If you prefer a rum punch, leave out the Herb enhancement and add some nice Jamaican rum instead. You can find dried sorrel online or in Caribbean markets.

CHILLED SORREL PUNCH

MAKES FOUR 6-OUNCE SERVINGS (5 MG THC PER SERVING)

¾ cup dried sorrel (hibiscus flower sepals)

2-inch piece fresh ginger, sliced crosswise into rounds

1 orange, thinly sliced into rounds

6 allspice berries

3 whole cloves

1 cinnamon stick

3 cups boiling water

½ cup honey

2 cups bite-size pieces fruit: peaches, nectarines, pineapples, mango, raspberries, strawberries, or blackberries

¾ cup rum (preferably Jamaican rum) or 2 teaspoons CannaVanilla Extract (page 29)

4 large fresh mint sprigs

1. Combine the sorrel, ginger, orange slices, allspice berries, cloves, and cinnamon stick in a large heatproof bowl. Cover with boiling water and set aside to cool to room temperature, then cover the bowl with plastic wrap and refrigerate the mixture overnight.

2. The next day, strain the mixture through a fine-mesh sieve into a bowl or large pitcher. Use a spoon to press on the solids to extract as much liquid as possible. Discard the solids.

3. Stir the honey into the sorrel tea, then add the fruit and rum or CannaVanilla. Divide among 4 wineglasses. Use a slotted spoon to add some fruit to each glass and serve with a mint sprig.

VARIATION: WARM SORREL PUNCH

If you'd like to serve the punch warm, after straining the mixture in step 2, return it to a clean saucepan and warm over medium heat. Remove from the heat and stir in the rum or CannaOil and the cut-up fruit. Divide the fresh fruit from the saucepan among 4 mugs, top off with the punch, and serve with a strip of orange peel and a cinnamon stick, if you like.

TONICS, HERBS, AND GOOD-FOR-YOU CURES

Dried Herb was an ingredient in many of the folk remedies and home cures my mother used to make. She used Herb steeped in tea when she was feeling nauseated or for aches and cramps and sometimes steep some Herb with aloe vera or add Herb to tea for an evening relaxation brew. For us kids, right before the beginning of a new school week, on a Sunday, or just because Mommy thought we needed it, we got served up a glass of the boiled-up bark, Herb, and roots, concoctions our family called "tonics" (made without Herb, of course!). The elders believed these tonics would help clean our blood of impurities, help digestion, and give our bodies an overall good cleanse. Mommy liked to add super bitter leaves of cerasee (an herb that grows throughout the Caribbean and also in Florida) to help us detox from too much junk food that we would have at school, or leaf of life to help with headaches or to clean out our system. At home, I make my family juices and smoothies rather than traditional Jamaican tonics—they just taste a whole lot better! Fresh ginger helps calm a stomach; spirulina (a green algae powder) offers protein and B vitamins, which are so important for vegetarians who don't get them from animal sources; and fresh turmeric assists digestion. Of course kale, carrots, citrus juice, and berries all factor in too as does anything that grows in my garden from mangoes to aloe vera.

DADDY AND MOMMY were big-time juicers, always turning papayas, pineapples, passion fruits, tamarind, and star fruit into refreshing and healthful tonics for our family. Well before green juice was a thing, Daddy said drinking green juice is good for you and cleans your blood—he was, like, thirty years ahead of his time! He'd put cucumber and leafy greens such as callaloo and mint and sometimes linseed (flaxseed) in the blender with a little honey to sweeten it up. I omit the linseed (it's not my favorite flavor, but if you like the taste of flaxseeds or flaxseed oil, add a bit to the juice for extra nutrition) and add kale instead of callaloo (which can be hard to find) for a supergreen juice. If you live in a state where you can grow Herb, add a handful of fresh, green Herb leaves to the juice too—you won't get the THC effects since the juice isn't heated, but you will get the health benefits from the leaves, like antioxidants (see page 86 for more information)!

MARLEY FAMILY GREEN JUICE

MAKES FOUR 8-OUNCE SMOOTHIE-STYLE SERVINGS
OR TWO 8-OUNCE JUICE-STYLE SERVINGS (5 MG THC PER SERVING)

1½ cups chunks fresh pineapple (about ⅓ of a medium pineapple)

1 large cucumber, chopped

1 medium green apple, cored and chopped

6 Tuscan (lacinato) kale or Swiss chard leaves, central ribs removed, leaves roughly chopped (about 2 packed cups)

Leaves from 4 fresh mint sprigs

Leaves from 3 fresh flat-leaf parsley sprigs

⅓ to ½ cup fresh green cannabis leaves if you can get them (optional)

1 tablespoon cane sugar (optional)

Juice of 1 lime

3 ice cubes

1 to 2 teaspoons CannaOil (page 25), preferably made with coconut oil

1. Add to a blender in this order: pineapple, cucumber, apple, kale, mint, parsley, herb leaves (if using), sugar (if using), lime juice, and ice cubes.

2. If making smoothies: Add ¼ cup water and 2 teaspoons CannaOil and blend until smooth, adding a splash or two more water if needed. Pour into glasses and serve.

If making juice: Add ¼ cup of water and blend until smooth. Strain the mixture through a fine-mesh sieve into a bowl and stir in 1 teaspoon CannaOil. Pour into glasses and serve.

I BEGIN EVERY DAY with this spirulina smoothie. Spirulina is a protein- and iron-rich blue-green algae that gives me a natural and filling boost. I add it to a smoothie just like adding protein powder. Frozen blueberries help chill the drink without diluting it; if using fresh blueberries, you will probably want to add a few more ice cubes. Especially when Herb enhanced, this is a great way to mellow out post-workout while still feeling replenished and healthy.

CEDELLA'S SPIRULINA
SMOOTHIE

MAKES TWO 8-OUNCE SERVINGS (5 MG THC PER SERVING)

1 cup hulled and halved fresh or frozen strawberries

1 cup fresh or frozen pineapple chunks

1 banana

¾ cup fresh or frozen blueberries (if using fresh, increase the amount of ice cubes)

1 tablespoon honey

2 teaspoons spirulina powder

1 teaspoon CannaOil (page 25)

4 ice cubes

Add to a blender in this order: strawberries, pineapple, banana, blueberries, honey, spirulina powder, CannaOil, and ice cubes. Blend until smooth, stopping to stir and scrape down the blender jar if necessary. If you like it more like a juice than a smoothie, thin it out with cold filtered water. Divide between 2 glasses and serve.

THE NEXT SUPERFOOD

Order a fruity drink over ice or smoothie-style in Jamaica and chances are it'll have a silky, sexy richness that you can't quite put your finger on. That's Irish moss, a kind of seaweed known for adding a slick, thick texture to drinks. Irish moss was my Daddy's *air*—he'd get up in the morning and the first thing he'd ask was, "Where's my Irish moss?" He added it to juices to thicken them naturally and healthfully. Irish moss is filling too (kind of like chia seeds), making it a great way to refuel after working out or stall a hungry stomach between meals. Carrageenan, a common thickener, is actually extracted from Irish moss, which grows in reddish clumps on the rocks along the coastline of Jamaica and, according to Jamaicans, is known to have a stimulating effect on certain body parts (wink wink!). Other people say it's good for digestion and detox, so pick the benefit that suits you and go from there.

To use Irish moss, place 1 cup in a large bowl and cover it with room temperature water. Swish it around and lift it up so that any sand falls to the bottom of the bowl. Drain and repeat as needed until no more sand comes out. Fill a large saucepan with water and bring it to a boil over high heat. Reduce the heat to medium so the water gently simmers, add the Irish moss, and cook it until it is soft, about 10 minutes. Transfer the moss and about 1 cup of the cooking liquid to a blender and blend until smooth, adding more cooking liquid to thin the gel. I like it semigelatinous so it's easy to scoop; the gel will thicken as it cools. Store in an airtight container and add as much or as little to a juice or smoothie as you like (the blended Irish moss will keep for a couple of weeks).

MY PARENTS always used food to help keep me and my brothers and sisters healthy, but sometimes the treatments were hard to swallow. When we'd see Daddy coming with a glass of aloe vera juice we just wanted to run! He told us to drink it because it was good for our belly *and* our blood, but boy, did it taste awful. Afterwards he'd give us a chaser of something sweet, like this tangy juice with lime and ginger. Passion fruit has a great sour edge with a natural acidity that combines so nicely with pineapple and ginger. A little watermelon adds natural sweetness and that gorgeous sunrise color that brings me right back to being a kid and watching the sun come up over the ocean. Leave out the Herb enhancement and spike the juice with rum instead (preferably Jamaican rum, of course) for a cocktail.

PASSION JUICE

MAKES TWO 8-OUNCE SERVINGS (5 MG THC PER SERVING)

6 passion fruits

1½ cups watermelon chunks (1-inch)

1 cup fresh pineapple chunks (1-inch)

1-inch piece fresh ginger, peeled and roughly chopped

1 to 2 tablespoons honey (optional)

1 teaspoon CannaOil (page 25)

6 ice cubes

1. Place a fine-mesh sieve over a medium bowl. Slice the passion fruits in half and scoop the pulp and seeds into the sieve. Use a spoon to press on the pulp and seeds, extracting as much juice as possible. Discard the solids and pour the juice into a blender (you should end up with ⅓ to ½ cup).

2. Add the watermelon, pineapple, ginger, honey (if using), CannaOil, and ice cubes to the blender and blend until smooth, adding a splash or two of cold water if you want a thinner consistency. Divide the juice between 2 glasses and serve.

I WAS NAMED AFTER MY DADDY'S MOTHER, Cedella, and star fruit was her favorite fruit. Star fruit has a sweet-and-sour thing happening that makes it a nice, mellow mixer with the pungency of freshly juiced carrot, ginger, and lime. Sometimes we'd get a nice blend like this from Juicy, the juice man whose cart was—and still is—in front of Tuff Gong, my family's recording studio in Kingston, Jamaica. Juicy used to juice for Daddy, and he'll still juice for whoever comes his way. This juice contains a good amount of ginger to put some fire in your belly. Use less—or more!—as you like.

CATCH A STAR JUICE

MAKES FOUR 8-OUNCE SMOOTHIE-STYLE SERVINGS OR TWO 8-OUNCE JUICE-STYLE SERVINGS (5 MG THC PER SERVING)

1½ pounds star fruit, ends trimmed (4 to 6 star fruit depending on how big they are)

3-inch piece fresh ginger, peeled and roughly chopped

3 fingers fresh turmeric, peeled and roughly chopped (or ½ teaspoon ground turmeric)

⅔ cup fresh lemon or lime juice (or a combination of the two)

4 medium carrots, peeled and roughly chopped

1 cup ice water

3 to 4 tablespoons cane sugar, to taste

1 to 2 teaspoons CannaOil (page 25), made with coconut oil

1. Add to a blender in this order: star fruit, ginger, turmeric, lemon or lime juice, and carrots.

2. If making smoothies: Add the ice water, the sugar, and 2 teaspoons CannaOil and blend until smooth. Pour into glasses and serve.

   If making juice: Add the ice water and blend until smooth. Strain the mixture through a fine-mesh sieve into a bowl and stir in 1 teaspoon CannaOil (the oil is added after straining so you don't waste any CannaOil in the discarded solid matter). Pour into glasses and serve.

3

ALL-DAY MUNCHIES!

*"I feel so high,
I even touch the sky,
above the falling rain."*
—"KAYA," BOB MARLEY

n our family, Herb represents healing—of a nation, of the spirit—so we have great respect when it comes to Herb. We use it to come together and feel uplifted and enlightened . . . but when I was a teenager, I was smoking to have fun and get high—and you know what happens oftentimes when you get high. . . . you get the munchies! Instead of scarfing down a bag of chips, why not let your eyes fall on something clean and good like Beet "Hummus" (page 107) or Hemp Guacamole (page 110)? I've chosen not to enhance the snacks in this chapter so that they can be counted on for easy eating without worrying about dosage and Herb intensity. I want you to be able to snack and be satisfied without worrying about getting more and more high. Since they aren't enhanced, these dips and munchies are excellent party add-ons and are great for bulking out Herb-inclusive menus with eats that your guests won't have to think twice about taking seconds of. If you do choose to enhance them with Herb (see box below), just be sure to preportion them into single-serving sizes so everyone can be carefree. We all know how hard it is to limit yourself to one serving of popcorn or guacamole once you get going (it tastes soooo good!).

SPIKE YOUR SNACKS

Because snacks by nature are a little difficult to preportion into single serving sizes I've deliberately kept all the snacks in this chapter free from Herb. (Plus they're so tasty, it's hard to stop with just a handful.) But it's easy to give your snacks a boost if you do want to. Any of the recipes in this chapter can be enhanced with CannaButter (page 26) or CannaOil (page 25) or, even easier, add a few shakes of cannaboosted seasoning to the snacks. Sprinkle Herb-Sesame Salt (page 48) over a bowl of steamed edamame, stir a teaspoon of boosted Jerk Seasoning (page 45) into your bean dip, or roast up sweet potato wedges tossed with olive oil and boosted Smoke Salt (page 47). Just make sure everyone partaking knows what constitutes a serving so they don't inadvertently overindulge.

MY DADDY BELIEVED IN THE CONCEPT OF LIFE ENERGY, and hemp seeds offer tons of it in the form of 10 grams of protein per serving of this dip. Hemp seeds (page 79) are a powerful superfood that also boast a full spectrum of amino acids, making it a complete protein. Add the benefits of folate from the avocado and the immune-boosting and antioxidant-rich garlic and you've got a snack that makes you feel like you can take on the world.

SUPERPOWERED HEMP DIP

SERVES 6 (MAKES 1½ CUPS)

1 cup hulled hemp seeds

1 medium garlic clove, roughly chopped

3 to 4 tablespoons fresh lemon juice (1 to 2 lemons)

2 to 3 tablespoons unflavored almond or soy milk

2 tablespoons finely chopped fresh basil

1 tablespoon finely chopped fresh flat-leaf parsley

1 tablespoon finely chopped fresh thyme

About 1 teaspoon fine sea salt

1 Hass avocado, halved and pitted

1 tablespoon coconut oil

Crackers, Homemade Pita Chips (page 107), or fresh vegetables, for serving

1. Place the hemp seeds in a food processor and process until the seeds break down into a thick paste, stopping to scrape the sides and bottom of the bowl as needed, until the mixture looks like soft clay, 2 to 3 minutes.

2. Add the garlic and 3 tablespoons of the lemon juice and process until well combined, about 1 minute. Add 2 tablespoons of the almond milk, the basil, parsley, thyme, and salt. Scoop in the avocado and process until combined. Taste and adjust for salt, adding more almond milk if the mixture is too thick and a squeeze of lemon juice if you'd like the dip tangier. Pulse in the coconut oil.

3. Serve with crackers, pita chips, or fresh vegetables.

VARIATION: HEMP GUACAMOLE

You can easily turn this into a protein-loaded guacamole with a few additions and substitutions: Pulse in a few scallions and fresh cilantro in place of the basil, parsley, and thyme. Add a chopped jalapeño or Scotch bonnet. Serve with the fried plantain chips (page 110).

WHEN I THINK OF CRAVINGS, the first thought that comes to mind is something that hits both the sweet and salty notes. This popcorn packs a bit of heat too, thanks to my homemade Jerk Seasoning and a good pinch of cayenne (there is already cayenne in the jerk seasoning, but I like a little extra). One of the first times I made this I included Spiked Jerk Seasoning and left it out on the counter. Wouldn't you know a friend went crazy on it (because it's so very delicious and you just can't stop eating it!) and ate about four servings—good thing he had a high tolerance for THC! If you're thinking of making this with CannaButter or Herb-spiked seasoning, I recommend preportioning the popcorn into bowls or bags because we all know how compulsive eating salty-sweet popcorn can be, and when it comes to edibles, portion control is key!

JAMMIN' CARAMEL-JERK POPCORN

SERVES 8

16 cups popped popcorn (from ½ cup kernels if making homemade)

1 stick plus 2 tablespoons (5 ounces) unsalted butter

½ cup lightly packed light brown sugar

¼ cup granulated cane sugar

Flaky sea salt

⅓ cup half-and-half or cream

1½ tablespoons Jerk Seasoning (page 45)

¼ to ½ teaspoon cayenne pepper

¼ teaspoon baking soda

Finely grated zest of 2 limes

1. Adjust one oven rack in the upper third of the oven and another in the lower third and preheat the oven to 250°F. Line 2 rimmed baking sheets with parchment paper. Place the popcorn in a large heatproof bowl.

2. Melt the butter in a medium saucepan over medium heat. Stir in both sugars and increase the heat to medium-high, stirring constantly. Once the mixture starts to bubble and boil, add a few pinches of salt and 3 tablespoons water. Cook, stirring constantly (scrape the bottom and into the corners of the pan too so nothing burns), until smoke comes off the sugar, about 3 minutes. Remove from the heat and immediately pour in

the half-and-half, jerk seasoning, cayenne, baking soda, and lime zest (the caramel will foam up thanks to the baking soda—don't worry, that's totally normal).

3. Pour the caramel over the popcorn while stirring with a heat-resistant spatula. Once it is evenly coated, divide it between the baking sheets.

4. Sprinkle the popcorn with a few generous pinches of flaky salt. Bake, stirring every 15 minutes, for 25 minutes. Switch the pans from top to bottom to top and continue baking and stirring until it is glossy and crisp, about 20 minutes longer. Remove from the oven, cool completely, and store in an airtight container for up to 1 week.

I USED TO GO CRAZY FOR STUFFED DUMPLINGS when I was a kid and now my children do too. Because they are extra satisfying, I find that they're a really smart add-on for dinner parties that are going to include dishes with Herb so everyone feels happy and full because they can eat as many fried dumplings as they want (and who wouldn't want to double up on that?). Leafy green callaloo, kind of like a cross between Swiss chard and spinach, is what we use for the filling in Jamaica, but you can substitute chopped fresh spinach or Swiss chard if you can't get fresh callaloo (canned callaloo just doesn't have the same texture or flavor). Or leave out the greens altogether for an all-out decadent cheesy dumpling.

CALLALOO AND SMOKY GOUDA FRIED DUMPLINGS

SERVES 8 (MAKES 16 DUMPLINGS)

DUMPLING DOUGH

2 cups all-purpose flour

1 teaspoon baking powder

½ teaspoon fine sea salt

1 tablespoon coconut oil

FILLING

2 cups packed fresh callaloo or baby spinach, roughly chopped

½ yellow onion, finely chopped

1 small plum tomato, finely chopped

1 large garlic clove, minced

½ Scotch bonnet pepper, finely chopped (seeded for less heat)

1 teaspoon finely chopped fresh thyme

¼ teaspoon fine sea salt

½ cup shredded smoked Gouda cheese

About 6 cups vegetable oil

Guava Ketchup (optional; page 114)

I. **MAKE THE DUMPLING DOUGH:** Whisk together the flour, baking powder, and salt in a large bowl. Add the oil and work it in with your fingertips until the mixture looks crumbly. Stir in ⅓ cup water, kneading the mixture until it comes together. Add more water, 1 tablespoon at a time, until you can knead the dough into an evenly textured ball without any dry patches (you may need to add up to 3 more tablespoons water depending on the dryness of your flour and the humidity of your kitchen).

(recipe continues)

2. **MAKE THE FILLING:** Add 2 tablespoons water to a medium nonstick skillet. Add the callaloo or spinach to the skillet followed by the onion, tomato, garlic, Scotch bonnet, thyme, and salt. Cover and cook over medium heat until the spinach is completely wilted, 2 to 3 minutes. Transfer the mixture to a colander and set in the sink to drain until completely cooled. Place the callaloo mixture in a bowl and stir in the grated smoked Gouda.

3. Pour 2 inches oil into a deep saucepan and heat to 375°F over medium-high heat.

4. While the oil heats, assemble the dumplings: Break off a tablespoon of dough and knead it with your thumbs until smooth, then roll it into a ball. Use your fingers and thumbs to flatten it into a thin 4-inch disk. Make the "OK" sign with the forefinger and thumb of your nondominant hand and place the dough on top of the "O." Press the dough into the "O" to make a little bowl, then add about ½ tablespoon of the filling. Gather the edges of the dough and pinch them together, sealing the dumpling shut. Repeat with the rest of the dough and the filling.

5. Add 4 to 5 dumplings to the hot oil (you don't want to overcrowd the pan or the temperature of the oil will drop, and instead of frying up crispy the dumplings will absorb the oil and be greasy). Fry them on all sides until golden brown, 2 to 3 minutes total. Use a slotted spoon or frying spider to transfer the dumplings to a plate lined with paper towels. Add more dumplings to the pan and repeat. Serve with Guava Ketchup, if desired.

HUMMUS IS ONE OF MY STAPLES. Here I substitute roasted beets for the chickpeas, just to change things up and give the dip the most stunning hot pink vibe. I like to roast a whole bunch of beets at once and keep them in the fridge for salads (I quick-pickle them for the salad on page 133), sandwiches, and just to snack on with a sprinkle of salt and maybe a little crumble of goat cheese. If your store carries vacuum-sealed roasted beets (or if they stock roasted beets in the salad bar), buy them. It makes whipping up hummus the simplest thing that you can cook up even on the craziest of days. While this version is Herb-free, you can easily enhance the recipe by adding 1 tablespoon CannaOil to the hummus—it's killer as a sandwich spread with some fresh mozzarella or packed into a small container with carrot sticks for dipping to bring along on a trip to the beach or to pack in a backpack for a day out and about.

FRESH BEET "HUMMUS"
WITH HOMEMADE PITA CHIPS

SERVES 6 (MAKES 1½ CUPS DIP)

HUMMUS

1 large beet, ends trimmed

1 tablespoon plus 1 teaspoon extra-virgin olive oil, plus extra for drizzling

½ cup tahini (sesame paste)

2 garlic cloves, smashed

¼ cup fresh lemon juice (1 to 2 lemons)

1½ teaspoons fine sea salt

1 tablespoon finely chopped fresh flat-leaf parsley

HOMEMADE PITA CHIPS

⅓ cup extra-virgin olive oil

3 garlic cloves, smashed

3 sprigs fresh rosemary

2 pita breads

2½ tablespoons Herb-Sesame Salt (page 48)

1. **ROAST THE BEET FOR THE HUMMUS:** Preheat the oven to 375°F.

2. Place the beet on a square of foil. Drizzle 1 teaspoon of the oil over the beet and wrap it tightly in the foil, then set the beet on a baking sheet. Roast the beet until a paring knife easily slips into the center, 50 minutes to 1 hour 15 minutes, depending on how big the beet is. (Leave the oven on for the pita chips, but reduce the temperature to 350°F.)

(recipe continues)

Open the foil and, once the beet is cool enough to handle, use a paring knife, your fingers, or a vegetable peeler to remove the skin (wear kitchen gloves if you're worried about staining your hands). Set aside while you make the pita chips.

3. **MAKE THE HERB PITA CHIPS:** Pour the olive oil into a small saucepan and add the smashed garlic and rosemary sprigs. Heat the oil over medium-high heat until the garlic is just starting to become golden, swirling the oil in the pan often, 4 to 5 minutes. Don't brown the garlic, or the oil will be bitter. Remove from the heat and transfer the mixture to a medium bowl to cool.

4. Slice each pita into 6 wedges, then separate the pieces so you end up with 12 triangles from each pita. Place the pita triangles rough-side up on a rimmed baking sheet and dab each with some of the herb oil and season generously with the Herb-Sesame Salt. Bake the pita chips until they are golden, rotating the pan front to back halfway through baking, 12 to 15 minutes. Remove from the oven and set aside to cool, then transfer the chips to a large bowl.

5. **MAKE THE HUMMUS:** Add the beet, remaining 1 tablespoon oil, tahini, garlic, lemon juice, salt, and 2 tablespoons water to a food processor and process until the mixture is thick and creamy. Taste and adjust with more salt if needed, and up to 2 more tablespoons water if the consistency is too thick. Use a rubber spatula to scrape the hummus into a medium bowl. Serve with the pita chips.

BABAGHANOUJ MASHUP

I make an easy stir-and-serve-style dip all the time for my boys. Soul will call me from college and ask me to send it to him, and when I go on tour with Skip, I'll make a batch for everyone on the road. It's creamy and spicy and great for dipping with fresh vegetables like carrots and bell pepper strips or with pita or tortilla chips, or even as a spread for a sandwich. Just stir together 1 cup of your favorite brand of prepared babaghanouj, 2 cups spicy tomato salsa, 3 minced garlic cloves, 8 pitted and chopped black olives, 2 tablespoons roughly chopped capers, a healthy pinch of chopped fresh basil, and as much of your favorite hot sauce—my favorite is Catch a Fire (page 229) made with Scotch bonnets—as you can handle!

IN JAMAICA we had many neighborhood friends who often stopped by with armfuls of the mangoes, lychees, and citrus fruit that grew on their property. Remembering how our neighbors shared abundance always reminds me of my father's bright soul and his deep love of giving. Around my house in Miami, we are lucky to have quite a few avocado trees, although about half of the avocados go to the squirrels! It's okay though—sharing is caring and that's a beautiful thing.

GUACAMOLE
WITH FRIED PLANTAIN CHIPS

SERVES 4

PLANTAIN CHIPS

6 cups vegetable oil

2 green plantains

Fine sea salt or Garlic Salt (page 49), for sprinkling

GUACAMOLE

2 avocados, halved and pitted

Juice of 1 lime

¾ teaspoon fine sea salt

2 scallions, white and light green parts only, finely chopped

1 Scotch bonnet pepper, halved and finely chopped (seeded for less heat)

1 teaspoon Herb-Sesame Salt (optional; page 48)

2 tablespoons finely chopped fresh cilantro leaves (optional)

1. **FRY THE PLANTAIN CHIPS:** Heat the oil to 375°F in a medium saucepan over medium-high heat.

2. Meanwhile, slice the ends off of the plantains. Use a knife to make a slit down each plantain from one end to the other, then remove the peels. Cut the plantains at a slight angle into 1/16-inch-thick slices.

3. Add about one-quarter of the plantain slices to the hot oil and fry until golden brown and crisp on both sides, using a slotted spoon or frying spider to turn them often, 1½ to

(recipe continues)

2 minutes. Transfer them to a plate lined with paper towels and sprinkle with salt or Garlic Salt. Repeat with the remaining plantains, frying them in batches.

4. **MAKE THE GUACAMOLE:** Use a spoon to scoop the avocados into a medium bowl. Add the lime juice and salt and smash with a fork until smooth. Stir in the scallions and Scotch bonnet. If using, stir in the Herb-Sesame Salt and cilantro. Scrape the guacamole into a serving bowl and serve with the plantain chips.

HOW I TALK TO MY KIDS ABOUT HERB

It should go without saying that Herb—whether you cook with it, soak in it (page 224), or smoke it—is for adults only. In states where Herb is legal, you have to be over the age of twenty-one to buy or possess Herb. Generally speaking, as long as Herb is being used responsibly and for healing purposes (of body or mind), I'm all for it. I've had conversations about Herb with my two older sons, Skip and Soul Rebel. I've explained to them that the high can be nice, or it can be bad. They need to make sure they know from whom they are getting Herb and how it is grown. The last thing I want them to do is get wacky weed from a wacky place and have a bad experience. As a parent I have responsibilities too—like always making sure anything that has Herb in it is clearly labeled—not just with what is inside, but with how much THC is in a serving. This is a good practice whether you have kids or not! Keep Herb-enhanced foods out of childrens' reach just as you would alcohol, and please do be responsible with what you make and how and where it is stored.

GUAVA AND YUCA are both typical Caribbean ingredients, and they taste wonderful together. Here the yuca is roasted in the oven like steak fries. My homemade Smoke Salt (page 47) gets sprinkled over them before serving for a killer barbecue-like taste alongside the guava-based ketchup. The ketchup batch doubles easily—I love it on a veggie burger (page 167) or served with the Callaloo and Smoky Gouda Fried Dumplings (page 104).

SMOKY BAKED YUCA WEDGES
WITH GUAVA KETCHUP

SERVES 4 (MAKES 1½ CUPS GUAVA KETCHUP)

GUAVA KETCHUP

1¼ cups guava juice

½ cup distilled white vinegar

¼ cup tomato puree

2 tablespoons molasses

8 dry-packed sun-dried tomatoes halves
   (not oil-packed)

½ white onion, roughly chopped

3 garlic cloves, smashed

2 pieces crystallized ginger

½ teaspoon ground allspice

⅛ teaspoon ground cinnamon

1 fresh thyme sprig

½ teaspoon fine sea salt

1 Scotch bonnet pepper, pricked 2 times
   with a fork

YUCA WEDGES

2 pounds yuca

2 teaspoons fine sea salt

2 tablespoons coconut oil

2 teaspoons Smoke Salt (page 47),
   or store-bought smoked salt

I. **MAKE THE GUAVA KETCHUP:** Combine the guava juice, vinegar, tomato puree, molasses, sun-dried tomato halves, onion, garlic, ginger, allspice, cinnamon, thyme, and sea salt in a medium saucepan. Bring the mixture to a simmer over medium-high heat, stirring often, then reduce the heat to medium-low and add the Scotch bonnet. Simmer gently, stirring occasionally, until the sauce is thick and the flavors have come together, about 30 minutes. Remove from the heat to cool for 20 minutes.

2. Fish out the Scotch bonnet and discard (if you want your ketchup extra spicy, leave it in) and transfer the mixture to a blender. Blend until smooth. Scrape the ketchup into an airtight container and refrigerate. It will keep refrigerated for up to 2 weeks.

3. **MAKE THE YUCA WEDGES:** Preheat the oven to 450°F.

4. Bring a large saucepan of water to a boil. Slice off the ends of each yuca, then use a vegetable peeler to peel off the tough skin. Slice each yuca in half crosswise if needed so it fits in the pan (if your yuca is small, don't worry about it). Add the salt and boil for 15 minutes. Drain the yuca and pat with paper towels, then quarter it lengthwise, slice away the tough core, and slice the pieces lengthwise (so they look like thick-cut steak fries).

5. Transfer the yuca wedges to a large bowl and toss with the coconut oil and Smoke Salt, then transfer to a rimmed baking sheet. Roast for 15 minutes, then use a spatula to turn them. Roast until browned, crisp, and tender, about 15 minutes longer. Remove from the oven and transfer to a plate. Serve with the Guava Ketchup.

FOR THE LOVE OF BAMMY

Yuca is not just for fries. In Jamaica yuca (called cassava on the island) is the basis for one of our most beloved foods, the bammy. Along with fried dumplings and festival, bammy is one of Jamaica's staple starches, and we eat it for breakfast or dinner, with fish, veggies or solo as a snack. These flatbreads are made from yuca that has been grated, rinsed, dried, and salted to create a flour, and they go back to the time of Jamaica's native Arawak people. These thick, pancake-sized flatbread are usually soaked in coconut milk and then pan-fried, deep-fried, or steamed until golden-crisp on the outside (if frying) and tender and soft on the inside. It's possible to make bammy at home but the process is not fast or simple. For those reasons most Jamaicans satisfy their craving for bammy at food stalls on the street. It's one of the first things I look for when I go back to visit.

CRUNCHY, COLORFUL, SALTY, AND BRINY, homemade pickles are easy to make and are a vibrant and delicious addition to just about any meal—even breakfast! Just pack your veggies in a jar and pour the brine right over them. Here I use classic escovitch vegetables like onion, red bell pepper, and carrots to make the pickle, but you can pickle just about anything—green beans, carrots, cucumbers, And when you use up the pickles, don't toss the brine! Use it like vinegar to make salad dressings or drizzle over grilled vegetables. A few pickles in a pita with Beet "Hummus" (page 107) and herb-infused Island Potato Salad (page 181) makes for a great picnic lunch or easy outdoor concert bring-along dinner.

PICKLE ME THIS, PICKLE ME THAT

MAKES 1 QUART

1 small red onion, halved and each half thinly sliced lengthwise

2 large carrots, peeled and cut crosswise at an angle into ¼-inch-thick slices

1 medium cucumber, cut crosswise at an angle into ¼-inch-thick slices

1 medium red bell pepper, halved and sliced lengthwise into ½-inch-wide strips

1 cup bite-size cauliflower florets

1 to 3 Scotch bonnet peppers (depending on how spicy you want the pickle), halved and thinly sliced

¼ cup sugar

3 garlic cloves, thinly sliced

2 tablespoons kosher salt

1 teaspoon allspice berries

1¼ cups distilled white vinegar

1. Add the onion, carrots, cucumber, bell pepper, cauliflower, and Scotch bonnet to a 1-quart jar or four 8-ounce jars.

2. Combine 1 cup water, the sugar, garlic, salt, and allspice berries in a medium saucepan. Bring to a boil. Add the vinegar, return the liquid to a boil, then reduce the heat to medium-low and simmer 2 minutes. Pour the hot brine over the vegetables (the brine should completely cover them). Cover the jar and set aside to cool for 20 minutes.

3. Refrigerate for at least 1 day before using, and up to 3 weeks.

CRISPY ON THE OUTSIDE and moist in the middle, saltfish fritters are traditionally eaten at breakfast in Jamaica, but I think they're an ideal snack or party bite. Like the Callaloo and Smoky Gouda Fried Dumplings (page 104), they make a really fun add-on for herb-spiked dinner parties (see some sample menus on pages 56–57). Saltfish is essentially salt-preserved fillets of fish, usually cod, hake, or pollack. They can be found in most grocery stores, as well as Caribbean markets and health food stores. Before using in a recipe, you must soak the fillets to remove most of the salt, otherwise whatever you cook will be inedible! Many people soak the fish for 24 hours, changing the water every 4 hours or so, but a nice little island trick is to scald the fish instead—just drop the saltfish in boiling water and cook, covered, for 20 minutes. It's how we always did it in my home and is much faster and easier than the soaking method. You can easily double this recipe for a party and you can always spike the dipping sauce with Herb if you want to give this dish a boost.

SALTFISH FRITTERS
WITH FIERY DIPPIN' SAUCE

SERVES 4 (MAKES 12 FRITTERS)

FRITTERS

½ pound saltfish (salt cod)

¾ cup all-purpose flour

1½ teaspoons garlic powder

½ teaspoon cayenne pepper

½ teaspoon fine sea salt

2 scallions, very finely chopped

½ medium tomato, finely chopped

½ small green bell pepper, minced

½ small red bell pepper, minced

1 tablespoon finely chopped fresh thyme
  leaves

1 Scotch bonnet pepper, seeded and finely
  chopped

¼ cup vegetable oil, plus more as needed

FIERY DIPPIN' SAUCE

1 cup whole-milk or 2% plain Greek yogurt

1 tablespoon mayonnaise (optional)

1 teaspoon finely chopped canned chipotle
  peppers in adobo

Grated zest of ½ lime plus 1 to 2 tablespoons
  lime juice

1 to 2 teaspoons hot sauce (preferably
  Scotch bonnet–based)

2 tablespoons chopped fresh basil

¼ teaspoon fine sea salt

1. **MAKE THE FRITTERS:** Bring a large pot of water to a boil. Add the saltfish, reduce the heat to medium, set a cover halfway on the pot, and "scald" the fish at a gentle simmer for 20 minutes. Drain the fish, dry it between paper towels, pressing firmly to extract as much water as possible. Remove the skin and bones (if there are any) and finely chop the fish into small bits.

2. Whisk together the flour, garlic powder, cayenne, and salt in a medium bowl. Add the scallions, tomato, bell peppers, thyme, and Scotch bonnet. Stir in ⅔ cup water to create a batter with the consistency of a slightly runny pancake batter. Stir in the chopped fish.

3. Heat the oil in a large skillet over medium-high heat. Use a soup spoon to add some batter to the pan, using the underside of the spoon to pat it flat. Fry until golden, about 4 minutes. Turn the fritter over and fry on the other side until the center of the fritter resists light pressure, about 4 minutes more. Transfer the fritters to a plate lined with paper towels while you fry the remaining batter (add more oil if needed).

4. **MAKE THE FIERY DIPPIN' SAUCE:** Stir together the yogurt, mayonnaise (if using), chipotle, lime zest, 1 tablespoon of the lime juice, 1 teaspoon of hot sauce, the basil, and salt in a medium bowl. Taste and add more lime juice or hot sauce if needed. Serve the fritters with the sauce on the side.

4

||||||||||||||||||||||||||||||||||||||

FRESH AND
GREEN

"Sun is shining,
the weather is sweet now/
Make you wanna move your
dancing feet, yeah"

—"SUN IS SHINING," BOB MARLEY

resh fruit, salads, and raw vegetables make me feel my best—so vital and alive. Herb is totally natural as well, and when you buy it grown well with love and care, it can be used like medicine. That's why I especially like to enhance salads and fresh, vibrant foods with Herb. It just feels like I'm getting a double dose of good—from the built-in vitamins and minerals of the fruits and vegetables to the healthy antioxidants and healing properties (page 86) of the Herb. Whenever you're growing anything for consumption, whether it's Herb or carrots or chiles, you want to keep your garden natural, pesticide-free, and healthy. If you live where it's legal to grow Herb, you can use different plants as natural pest deterrents in your "Herb" garden—like basil, garlic, mint, and chiles. Herb likes all kinds of different growing conditions, from humid sea-bound islands to sunny valleys and lush backyard gardens—Herb is amenable to all kinds of situations! When I feel the need to re-balance and re-center, I go to my garden, pick what looks good, and head to the kitchen to make these recipes. They feed my soul, body, and spirit.

JERK CHICKEN (page 141) is an island staple, but as a vegetarian, I opt to marinate vegetables in jerk paste instead and throw them on the grill for a smoky-satisfying flavor. When I'm making a platter of jerk chicken for a party, I'll make a giant platter of these vegetables too as an excellent option for anyone who chooses not to eat meat. It's also just a fun way to give your veggies a hit of big flavor. Here I serve the vegetables over a green salad, but you can serve them on their own as a side dish, a main course with Gungo Rice 'n Peas (page 185), or stuff the veggies into a pita with some hummus (page 107) for a healthy sandwich.

GRILLED JERK VEGETABLES
WITH LIME VINAIGRETTE

SERVES 6 (5 MG THC PER SERVING)

GRILLED VEGETABLES

¼ cup Jerk Paste (page 46)

2 tablespoons extra-virgin olive oil

2 portobello mushrooms, stemmed

1 medium zucchini, halved lengthwise

1 Japanese eggplant, halved lengthwise

1 red bell pepper, halved and seeded

1 medium red onion, quartered (don't trim the root end so the onion quarters stay intact on the grill)

LIME VINAIGRETTE

Juice of 2 limes (about ¼ cup)

½ teaspoon fine sea salt

3 tablespoons extra-virgin olive oil

6 cups greens, such as baby spinach, arugula, chopped romaine or leaf lettuce

1 tablespoon finely chopped fresh Herbs (optional), such as basil, mint, tarragon, or parsley

1. **MARINATE THE VEGETABLES:** Mix the jerk paste and olive oil together in a large bowl. Add the portobello mushrooms, zucchini, eggplant, bell pepper, and onion and toss to coat. Set aside for at least 1 hour and up to overnight to marinate (if marinating more than a few hours, cover the bowl with plastic wrap and refrigerate the vegetables).

2. Make a medium-hot fire in a charcoal grill or heat a gas grill to medium-high. Grease the grill grates using grilling tongs and a paper towel dipped into oil, then place the

(recipe continues)

vegetables on the grill. Grill the vegetables on all sides until they are nicely charred and have grill marks (you may need to move the eggplant and portobellos to a cooler part of the grill so they can cook through without burning). Transfer the vegetables to a cutting board and slice them into bite-size pieces.

3. **MAKE THE SALAD:** Whisk the lime juice, salt, and olive oil together in a large bowl. Add the greens and toss to combine, then transfer to a large platter. Top with the grilled vegetables, sprinkle with Herbs (if using), and serve.

SHAKE IT UP, GIVE IT AWAY

Salad dressings and sauces are such a natural fit for an Herb enhancement because the CannaOil effortlessly blends into the oil component of the dressing—just like that, you have a medicated topping for your leafy greens and colorful veggies. Make triple the recipe for the dressing (use the one on page 123 for a guideline) or a sauce for your pasta. For a host gift, it can be fun to double or triple a batch of what you're serving, then divide the extra into glass jars. Be sure to tell them to keep the dressing or sauce refrigerated until they plan on using it—and let them know when to use it by. Also, always label the jar so people know how much THC the sauce contains in total and per serving. Also put a fun sticker or label on the jar so everyone knows it is medicated!

IF WHEN YOU THINK "EDIBLES" your brain goes straight to sweets, this can be a total Herb game changer. The Herb is added to the dressing for the kale, making this superclean and healthy salad something you can try out for an enhanced breakfast, at lunch, or alongside dinner. It's so nourishing and hearty, making it a nutritious start to a day of exercise, hiking, or plain good green eating. This is the kind of salad that you could modify in a bunch of ways: Take out the apple and add shredded chicken or tofu or some crumbled feta cheese; add some toasted sunflower seeds or pistachios, or even roasted vegetables. But don't lose the pickled red onions . . . they're my favorite part!

HEMP, KALE, AND APPLE SALAD

SERVES 4 (5 MG THC PER SERVING)

½ small red onion, thinly sliced

2 teaspoons distilled white vinegar

¾ teaspoon plus a pinch of kosher salt

3 tablespoons plus 1 teaspoon extra-virgin olive oil

2 teaspoons CannaOil (page 25)

1 small garlic clove

Juice of ½ lemon

1½ bunches Tuscan (lacinato) kale, central ribs removed, leaves sliced into thin ribbons (about 7 cups)

1 crisp apple, halved, cored, and cut into thin matchsticks

2 cups baby spinach or other tender leafy greens

¼ cup hulled hemp seeds

1. Toss the red onion, vinegar, and salt together in a small bowl and set aside.

2. Whisk together the olive oil, CannaOil, garlic, lemon juice, and a pinch of salt in a large bowl. Add the kale and toss to combine, then use your hands to massage the kale, squeezing and releasing it until the leaves darken in color and become tender, 1 to 2 minutes.

3. Add the apple matchsticks, baby spinach, and onion to the kale and toss to combine. Add most of the hemp seeds, toss to combine, then serve sprinkled with the remaining hemp seeds.

I'VE ALWAYS HAD A THING FOR MANGOES, especially East Indian mangoes. I swear, I could eat one every day. In Jamaica some people eat the skin and all, just like an apple. Here, slightly underripe mangoes about'a turn ripe give this refreshing salad a sweet-sour crunch. It's just loaded with beautiful flavors and textures, especially if you sprinkle the Herb-Sesame Salt over the top before serving. You could even serve this for dessert by cutting out the shallot (or onion) and the sesame salt and substituting a sprinkle of coarse sugar instead.

"ABOUT'A TURN" MANGO
SALAD

SERVES 4 (5 MG THC PER SERVING)

1 tablespoon distilled white vinegar

2 teaspoons CannaOil (page 25) or olive oil (if using sesame salt enhanced with herb)

Juice of ½ lime

½ teaspoon fine sea salt

½ large shallot or ½ small red onion, thinly sliced lengthwise

1 teaspoon finely chopped Scotch bonnet pepper

1 semiripe (mostly green) mango "about'a turn," peeled and ends cut off

¼ cup coarsely chopped fresh mint leaves

Herb-Sesame Salt (optional; page 48)

1. Whisk together the vinegar, oil, lime juice, and sea salt in a medium bowl. Add the shallot and Scotch bonnet and stir to combine.

2. Stand the mango upright and slice down from top to bottom and as close to the pit as possible to remove 1 lobe. Turn the mango and repeat on the other side. Follow the curve of the pit to remove the fruit from the sides. Discard the pit and cut the mango into ¼-inch-thick strips. Add the mango and mint to the bowl and toss to combine.

3. Cover the salad with plastic wrap and refrigerate for at least 30 minutes or overnight for the flavors to come together. Sprinkle with Herb-Sesame Salt before serving, if you like.

THERE ARE SO MANY FLAVOR AND TEXTURE CONTRASTS HERE—the flaky sweetness of coconut against the juicy-cool of mango, the earthy spice of curry, heat of habanero, the freshness of lime, scallion, and mint. It's a great make-ahead and bring-along kind of thing and is just the kind of dish you can make and then take to your next book group meeting to really get the conversation to a deeper level. Jamaican curry powder is a little mellower than traditional Indian curry powder, but if Indian curry is all you've got, go for it. My brother Ziggy makes an incredible curry-infused coconut oil (see page 229) that I love using in dishes like this.

QUINOA WITH CURRY CASHEWS AND COCONUT

SERVES 4 (5 MG THC PER SERVING)

¾ cup quinoa

¼ teaspoon plus a pinch fine sea salt

1 tablespoon coconut oil

¾ cup cashews

¾ cup unsweetened coconut flakes

2 teaspoons Jamaican curry powder

2 teaspoons CannaOil (page 25)

1 ripe mango, peeled and ends cut off

2 scallions, finely chopped

½ habanero pepper, finely chopped (seeded for less heat), or a Fresno chile

¼ cup finely chopped fresh mint leaves

Juice of 1 large lime

1. Place the quinoa in a medium bowl and cover with cold water. Swish around with your fingers, then drain through a fine-mesh sieve and run the quinoa under cold water. Bring 1 cup plus 2 tablespoons water plus ¼ teaspoon of the salt to a boil in a medium saucepan. Add the quinoa, return to a boil, then cover and reduce the heat to low. Cook until the quinoa is tender, has unspiraled, and has absorbed all of the water, about 25 minutes. Spread the quinoa on a rimmed baking sheet or a cutting board to cool.

2. Heat the coconut oil in a large skillet over medium-low heat. Add the cashews and cook, stirring often, until they become golden, 4 to 5 minutes. Add the coconut flakes, curry

(recipe continues)

powder, CannaOil, and the remaining pinch of salt. Continue to cook, stirring often, until the coconut is toasted, 1 to 2 minutes. Transfer the cashew mixture to a plate to cool.

3. Stand the mango upright and slice down from top to bottom and as close to the pit as possible to remove 1 lobe. Turn the mango and repeat on the other side. Follow the curve of the pit to remove the fruit from the sides. Discard the pit and cut the mango into bite-size pieces. Add the mango to a large bowl along with the quinoa, scallions, habanero, mint, and lime juice. Stir to combine.

4. Scatter the cashew mixture over the salad and serve.

HERB, FRUIT, AND VEGGIES: GARDENING FOR WELLNESS

Gardening—like Herb—is a proven stress reducer that can help with overall positivity. I am all for any activity that can bring you up in a natural, healthy way, and digging in my garden always makes me feel in touch and at one with nature and the life force of what is growing around me. At my home, I grow star fruit, chiles, all kinds of herbs, bananas, avocados, and so many papayas I can't even get rid of them all . . . and my mango trees are off the chain! The garden is full of the flavors that are important to my cooking— from thyme to scallions, Scotch bonnets to lemons and limes and lots of different varieties of mint. I'll go into the garden and pick a grapefruit or lychees for breakfast or a snack. I'll think about my day or reflect on a situation and try to channel my feelings into a positive place. Cooking for me isn't just about the act of getting something on the table—it's about the spirit of doing, from before I even plant the seed to the moment when I lift the fork.

IN THIS RATHER ELEGANT SALAD the tart sweet-sour taste of pickled beets works so nicely with creamy goat cheese and toasted pine nuts. For a nice presentation, leave the Herb out of the dressing and instead roll the log of goat cheese in an enhanced spice blend (pages 45 to 49). Slice the log and prop a couple of rounds against the spinach rather than crumbling the cheese over the salad.

SPINACH SALAD
WITH GOAT CHEESE, PICKLED BEETS, AND PINE NUTS

SERVES 4 (5 MG THC PER SERVING)

PICKLED BEETS

1 large beet, quartered (don't worry about peeling it)

½ cup apple cider vinegar

8 whole allspice berries

2 large garlic cloves, smashed

2 teaspoons cane sugar

1 teaspoon fine sea salt

2 fresh dill sprigs

SALAD

¼ cup pine nuts

2 tablespoons plus 1 teaspoon extra-virgin olive oil

2 teaspoons CannaOil (page 25)

1½ tablespoons fresh lemon juice

1 tablespoon finely chopped fresh dill, plus a little extra for serving

½ teaspoon fine sea salt

2 scallions, white and light green parts only, finely chopped

6 cups baby spinach

4 ounces fresh goat cheese

1. **PICKLE THE BEETS:** Bring a medium saucepan of water to a boil. Add the beet quarters and boil until a fork easily slides into a wedge, 20 to 25 minutes. Drain the beets and when cool, peel them and slice them crosswise into thin pieces.

(recipe continues)

2. While the beet cools, combine the vinegar, 3 tablespoons water, the allspice berries, garlic, sugar, and salt to a saucepan and bring to a simmer over medium-high heat, stirring occasionally to dissolve the sugar and salt. Remove from the heat and add the dill. Set aside to cool.

3. Place the beets in an airtight container and cover with the room temperature brine. Refrigerate for at least 2 hours, shaking the container every hour to redistribute the brine. (The pickled beets will keep for up to 1 week; you can actually store them longer in the fridge but they will continue to get softer in the brine.)

4. **MAKE THE SALAD:** Toast the pine nuts in a small skillet over medium heat, shaking the pan often, until they are golden brown, 4 to 6 minutes. Transfer the pine nuts to a plate and set aside to cool.

5. Whisk together the olive oil, CannaOil, lemon juice, dill, and salt in a large salad bowl. Stir in the scallions. Add the spinach and toss to combine. Scatter the pine nuts over the top. Scatter the beets over the greens and finish the salad by crumbling the goat cheese over the top. Sprinkle with a little dill and serve.

IF YOU CAN'T BEET 'EM . . . COOK 'EM

The leafy greens attached to beets are a tremendous source of vitamins and fiber, so why would you throw all that nutrition in the trash? Instead, chop and sauté them as you would Swiss chard or kale. A little oil, garlic, and salt is all they need, or you could add a sprinkle of Sesame Salt to give them a little cannaboost! They're also excellent added to a soup or a stew. So next time you buy beets be sure to buy them with the greens intact and look for bright, undamaged leaves with no yellowing or leathery spots for the most tender, flavorful dish. It's almost like getting a second vegetable for free!

5

|||||||||||||||||||||||||||||||||||

THE GET-
TOGETHER

"Quench me when I'm thirsty/
Come on and cool me down,
baby, when I'm hot/
Your recipe—darlin'—is so tasty/
When you show and stir your pot."

—"STIR IT UP," BOB MARLEY

hen you entertain with Herb, it's a time to let loose, throw your hands in the air, and celebrate. Most people tend to think of snacks and desserts as the most natural for infusing with THC, but I beg to differ. Infusing a main dish is a really smart way to include Herb in a menu because it's easy to control the dosage each guest receives when you portion out the servings. It can even be the *only* Herb-enhanced dish at a party—make all the starters, sides, and snacks Herb-free so the main dish can be the special guest star that no one can stop talking about! In this chapter, you'll find lots of recipes for fun and soulful foods. Choose the dish that best complements the mood you want for your gathering: A hearty lasagna is excellent for large groups or a comfy night in; bring macaroni and cheese to a Super Bowl party; and for any kind of outdoor party, grilled jerk chicken is a *must*. Growing up, home cooking was all I knew and the flavors of Jamaica—the curry, thyme, Scotch bonnet, scallion, ginger, and garlic—are still a big part of how I approach cooking today, so you'll find these bright and bold tastes in lots of the recipes whether they're more Jamaican like "fried fish and festival" or American like veggie burgers. No matter where the idea comes from, they're all comforting and full of flavor and spirit. When I need to feel close to home, these are the foods I come to again and again. A lot of these dishes are also great for potlucks—just make sure your host (and the guests) know that you mean *pot* luck literally!

I HAVE BEAUTIFUL MEMORIES of my mother buying big, pristine fresh fish from the fishermen on Bull Bay. My father would roast the fish on a sheet of zinc and then, when the fish was done, he'd walk it to the water and dip the fish in the sea for a salty, briny wash. Here, pan-seared snapper fillets get finished with a bath of sweet, sour, and a little spicy vinegar-based broth. Escovitch comes from the Spanish dish escabeche, but an escabeche is usually marinated for a bit, while the Jamaican version is served right away. Usually the fish is fried first, but I like to pan roast it for a healthier vibe.

SNAPPER ESCOVITCH

SERVES 4 (5 MG THC PER SERVING)

4 red snapper fillets (6 ounces each)

1 tablespoon canola oil

1 teaspoon plus a few pinches fine sea salt

1 cup distilled white vinegar

10 allspice berries

1 small green bell pepper, thinly sliced

1 small red bell pepper, thinly sliced

1 small red onion, halved and thinly sliced

2 fresh thyme sprigs

1 Scotch bonnet pepper, seeded and sliced

2 teaspoons CannaOil (page 25)

2 limes, quartered, for serving

1. With a sharp knife, score several diagonal lines into the skin side of each fish fillet, barely going ¼ inch deep (this helps keeps the fillet flat when pan-searing).

2. Heat the oil in a large nonstick skillet over medium-high heat. Set the fish in the skillet, skin-side down, and season the flesh side of the fish with a few pinches of salt. Cook until the skin is crisp, 4 to 5 minutes, then turn the fish over and cook on the other side until the fillets are cooked through, 3 to 5 minutes longer.

3. Transfer the fish to a platter and cover to keep warm. Add the vinegar and allspice to the skillet. Once it comes to a simmer, reduce the heat to medium and add the green and red bell peppers and the 1 teaspoon salt. Cook, stirring occasionally, for 1 minute, then add the red onion and thyme sprigs. Cook, stirring occasionally, until the peppers start to become tender, about 3 minutes. Add the Scotch bonnet and CannaOil and continue to cook for 2 minutes longer. Remove from the heat.

4. Pour the sauce over the fish and discard the thyme. Serve with the lime wedges.

YOU'RE DEFINITELY GOING TO GET INVITED TO A LOT MORE PARTIES if you show up with a platter of Herb-boosted jerk chicken. Is there any dish at all better for an outdoor summer gathering? I think not. The smell of spicy jerk chicken grilling away stokes the appetite like no other (even if you don't eat meat!). I make sure to buy chicken that was raised in humane and healthy conditions so I can feel good about what I am giving my guests to put into their bodies. You can also grill up some jerk vegetables (page 123) or serve plain vegetables with the extra barbecue sauce for your vegetarian friends.

GRILLED JERK CHICKEN WITH TAMARIND BARBECUE SAUCE

SERVES 4 (5 MG THC PER SERVING), WITH LEFTOVER BARBECUE SAUCE

JERK CHICKEN

1 tablespoon plus 1 teaspoon extra-virgin olive oil or coconut oil

1 tablespoon CannaOil (page 25); see Note

4 garlic cloves, minced

2 tablespoons Jerk Seasoning (page 45)

¼ teaspoon fine sea salt

4 bone-in, skin-on chicken thighs

4 organic chicken drumsticks

TAMARIND BARBECUE SAUCE

2 tablespoons coconut oil

1 medium red onion, quartered

3 garlic cloves, smashed

1 tablespoon grated fresh ginger

2 tablespoons chili powder

1 tablespoon smoked paprika

2 teaspoons fine sea salt

1 teaspoon freshly ground black pepper

¼ cup tomato paste

1 can (14 ounces) diced tomatoes (with juices)

3 tablespoons tamarind concentrate

2 tablespoons Dijon mustard

2 tablespoons honey

2 tablespoons molasses

2 tablespoons dark brown sugar

1 Scotch bonnet pepper, roughly chopped

1. **MARINATE THE CHICKEN:** Whisk the oil, CannaOil, garlic, salt, and jerk seasoning together in a large bowl. Add the chicken thighs and drumsticks and turn to coat evenly

(recipe continues)

with the mixture, cover the bowl with plastic wrap, and refrigerate for at least 8 hours or overnight.

2. **MAKE THE TAMARIND BARBECUE SAUCE:** Heat the coconut oil in a medium saucepan over medium-high heat. Add the onion and cook, stirring occasionally, until it starts to brown, 2 to 3 minutes. Reduce the heat to medium and stir in the garlic, ginger, chili powder, paprika, salt, and pepper and cook, stirring, until it is fragrant, about 30 seconds. Stir in the tomato paste and cook, stirring often, until the paste darkens, about 2 minutes, then deglaze the pan with ½ cup water, stirring and scraping any browned bits up from the bottom of the pan. Stir in the diced tomatoes, tamarind concentrate, mustard, honey, molasses, and brown sugar. Add the Scotch bonnet and reduce the heat to medium-low. Simmer gently, stirring occasionally, for 20 minutes.

3. Transfer the barbecue sauce to a blender. Carefully pulse once or twice to let off some steam, then blend until smooth. Return to the saucepan and continue to cook over medium-low heat, stirring occasionally, until the sauce reduces a little and thickens slightly, about 15 minutes. Pour 1 cup of barbecue sauce into a small bowl (refrigerate the rest of the barbecue sauce for up to 2 weeks, or freeze 1-cup portions in resealable freezer bags for up to 6 months).

4. Make a medium-hot fire in a charcoal or heat a gas grill to medium. Grease the grill grates using grilling tongs and a paper towel dipped into oil. Set the chicken on the grill skin-side down and cook until lightly charred on both sides, 12 to 16 minutes total. Brush the chicken on both sides with the sauce and continue to cook, turning and basting often, until the chicken is cooked through or an instant-read thermometer inserted into the thigh reads 160°F, about 8 minutes longer. Transfer to a platter and serve.

VARIATION: OVEN-BARBECUED CHICKEN

Prepare as above through step 3. Preheat the oven to 400°F and line a rimmed baking sheet with foil. Use a little oil to lightly grease the foil and place the chicken on the foil, skin-side up. Bake the chicken for 10 minutes, turn the pieces over, and continue baking for 5 minutes. Brush the chicken with the barbecue sauce, turn the pieces over, and brush the other side. Continue baking for 10 minutes. Preheat the broiler to high and adjust the oven rack to the upper third of the oven. Brush the chicken with the remaining barbecue sauce and broil it skin-side up until charred, 6 to 8 minutes (watch the chicken closely as broiler intensities vary). Transfer to a platter and serve.

NOTE Since the chicken probably won't absorb all of the THC from the CannaOil in the marinade, I use 1 tablespoon of the oil for 4 servings instead of 2 teaspoons. If you like, add some CannaOil to the leftover barbecue sauce (2 teaspoons for 4 servings) and serve it alongside the chicken for dipping.

EVEN THE NAME OF THIS RECIPE, unique to Jamaica, sounds like a party: Red Stripe battered fish 'n festival? Bring it on! This is a fun and different kind of meal to share with your guests—the fish is crispy and juicy, just like the best fish and chips, and the festival are like a sweeter, Jamaican take on hush puppies. Hellshire Beach, just outside of Kingston, is famous for having some of the best fried fish on the island. Thatched-roofed huts line the beach and all you need to do is walk past one and smell the fish frying to get that hunger pang deep down in the pit of your belly. The fish is fried up fresh to order and served with festival or bammies, a cassava root (yuca) pancake (page 115), on the side. I took the inspiration from the beach for this recipe, using Jamaica's beloved Red Stripe beer to make the batter for coating the fish. Since both the fish and festival are fried at high temperatures (which can dilute the potency of your Herb), the best way to introduce an herb component is through a dipping sauce. Be sure to name someone a designated fryer if you'll be partaking in the dish (or earlier courses)—you definitely don't want to start daydreaming while you're cooking oil is at 350°F! If you're the cook at the party, wait to partake until the pot of oil is off the fire.

RED STRIPE BATTERED
FISH 'N FESTIVAL

SERVES 4 (5 MG THC PER SERVING WITH THE DIPPING SAUCE)

3 cups all-purpose flour, plus extra for shaping

⅓ cup fine cornmeal

1½ teaspoons baking powder

¾ teaspoon fine sea salt

3 tablespoons granulated cane sugar

3 tablespoons unsalted butter, melted

½ teaspoon vanilla extract

6 cups neutral oil, for deep-frying

1 bottle (12 ounces) beer (preferably Red Stripe)

1½ pounds fish fillets (such as red snapper, ling cod, haddock, pollack, or tilapia), skin removed and sliced crosswise into 2-inch pieces

2 teaspoons CannaOil (page 25)

Hot sauce or Fiery Dippin' Sauce (page 119), for serving

2 lemons or limes (or a combination), cut into wedges

(recipe continues)

1. Whisk together 2½ cups of the flour, the cornmeal, baking powder, and salt in a medium bowl. Measure out ¾ cup of the mixture, transfer to another bowl, and stir in the remaining ½ cup flour. Set this mixture aside for making the fish batter.

2. To the flour mixture remaining in the first bowl, whisk in the sugar. In a small bowl or measuring cup, combine ⅔ cup cool water, the melted butter, and vanilla. Add the wet ingredients to the flour-sugar mixture, using a wooden spoon to stir until it comes together into a mass (add a tablespoon or two of water if the dough isn't coming together).

3. Turn the dough out onto a lightly floured work surface and knead until it comes together in a semismooth ball, about 1 minute. Wrap it in plastic wrap and set it aside to rest for 10 minutes.

4. Unwrap the dough and sprinkle it with a little flour. Divide the dough into 12 equal pieces and roll each into a 3- to 4-inch-long rope. Transfer to a plate, cover with plastic wrap, and set aside.

5. Heat the oil to 350°F in a large pot or Dutch oven over medium-high heat. Once the oil comes up to temperature, drop 4 to 5 pieces of festival into the oil and fry, turning often, until they are golden brown and cooked through, 6 to 8 minutes. Transfer to a wire rack and fry the remaining pieces.

6. Whisk the beer into the reserved bowl of flour and cornmeal, stirring until smooth. Dredge the fish fillets on both sides in the plain flour, then drop the fish into the batter to coat both sides, allowing the excess to drip back into the bowl. Immediately add to the hot oil, frying just a few pieces at a time and moving and turning them occasionally so they don't stick together. Fry the fish until golden brown on both sides and cooked through, 8 to 10 minutes (I like to take out a piece and cut into it to make sure the fish is cooked through before taking out the other fillets). Transfer to a wire rack. Repeat with the remaining fish.

7. Stir the CannaOil into the hot sauce and divide into 4 small dishes for dipping (one for each guest). Serve with lemons and limes on the side.

I CAN EAT PATTIES hot, cold, for breakfast, on a hike, as my dinner . . . you name it! The meat patty is like the Big Mac of Jamaica. It's the perfect way to pass out Herb in a fun, neat, and tidy package or tuck into your bag for the movies (hey, we all do it). You won't find many burger shops or pizza parlors on the island but patty shops are *everywhere*. I used to go with Daddy to a place in Half Way Tree in Kingston for patties. He loved them because they were a bit different, stuffed with corn and peas, and they fried their patties instead of baking them. I like mine on the more traditional side, except I stuff mine with a veggie mince (a crumbly ground meat substitute available in the freezer section where you find veggie burgers—or if you can't find it, just use crumbled veggie burger instead). The sign of a great patty is when you bite into it the filling almost bursts out of the sides, so don't hesitate to stuff these full up. The patty crust is made with coconut milk and curry powder, which gives it that trademark yellow color, but you can use store-bought pie dough or puff pastry instead if you're short on time. Use a 3- or 4-inch round cookie cutter to stamp out smaller pieces of dough for more party bites.

SPICY JAMAICAN PATTIES

MAKES 6 PATTIES (5 MG THC PER SERVING)

PASTRY

2 cups all-purpose flour, plus extra for rolling

2 teaspoons Jamaican curry powder

1½ teaspoons ground turmeric

½ teaspoon fine sea salt

½ cup chilled coconut oil (so it is solid)

7 to 8 tablespoons cold water

FILLING

2 tablespoons coconut oil

6 scallions, white and light green parts only, thinly sliced

½ medium green bell pepper, finely chopped

2 medium garlic cloves, minced

1½ teaspoons finely chopped fresh thyme

1 medium tomato, finely chopped

½ teaspoon plus a pinch fine sea salt

½ teaspoon freshly ground black pepper

1½ cups veggie crumbles or crumbled veggie burger (thawed if frozen)

1 Scotch bonnet pepper, finely chopped

1 tablespoon CannaOil (page 25)

1 large cage-free egg (optional)

(recipe continues)

1. **MAKE THE PASTRY:** Combine the flour, curry powder, turmeric, and salt in a food processor and pulse to combine. Add the solid coconut oil and pulse for eight 1-second pulses to work it into the dry ingredients. Transfer the mixture to a large bowl and add 7 tablespoons of the water, using your hands to bring the ingredients together into a smooth ball (add the extra tablespoon of water if the dough seems dry). Turn the dough out onto a large sheet of plastic wrap and knead 2 or 3 times to get it to come together, then press it into a round about ½ inch thick. Wrap in plastic and refrigerate for at least 30 minutes or up to 2 days.

2. **MAKE THE FILLING:** Heat 1 tablespoon of the coconut oil in a large skillet over medium-high heat. Add the scallions and bell pepper and cook, stirring occasionally, until they start to brown, 2 to 3 minutes. Stir in the garlic and cook until it is fragrant, about 30 seconds. Stir in the thyme, tomato, ½ teaspoon of the salt, and the black pepper. Reduce the heat to medium and cook until the mixture is thick and no liquid remains in the pan.

3. Add the veggie crumbles and Scotch bonnet and continue to cook, stirring often, until the crumbles are heated through and the mixture starts to brown, about 10 minutes. Stir in the CannaOil, then transfer the filling to a medium bowl and set aside to cool (if you use warm filling, the pastry will be too soft to shape).

4. Preheat the oven to 400°F. Line a baking sheet with parchment paper.

5. Take the dough out of the refrigerator and let it sit at room temperature for 5 to 10 minutes if it has been chilling for more than 30 minutes. Unwrap the dough and place it on a surface lined with plastic wrap or parchment paper. Sprinkle the top with a little flour and roll the pastry into a sheet ¼ to ⅛ inch thick. Use a 5½- to 6-inch-diameter bowl turned upside down to press 4 circles into the pastry. Then use a knife to cut out the rounds. Place the dough rounds on the lined baking sheet. Bring the scraps together and re-roll them, then cut out 2 more rounds for 6 total.

6. Whisk the egg (if using) with a pinch of salt and 1 tablespoon water in a small bowl. Place one-sixth of the filling on each pastry round, then brush the edges with egg wash, if using—otherwise just use water. Fold and press the edges together to seal. Use a fork to poke a few holes in the top of each patty, then use the fork to crimp the edges.

7. Brush the top of the patties with more egg wash (if using), then bake them for 10 minutes. Reduce the heat to 375°F and continue to bake until the patties are golden brown, 14 to 16 minutes longer. Remove from the oven and transfer to a wire rack to cool at least a few minutes before eating. (If making the patties ahead of time, reheat them in a 200°F oven for about 10 minutes before serving—just long enough to re-crisp the pastry crust.)

CREATIVE WAYS TO "POT"LUCK ON THE FLY

Not everyone has access to high-quality Herb or knows how to enhance a dish with Herb . . . but that doesn't mean that they can't contribute a dish to your Herb dinner party! Here are some simple ways to introduce Herb into already cooked food:

• IN A SAUCE: Just stir CannaOil (page 25) into a sauce. Pour the sauce into a measuring cup and divide it equally among your guests. For example, if your guests bring fried chicken, make some quick hot honey by whisking honey and hot sauce with some CannaOil (I like 5 mg THC per serving—following the instructions on page 26 and using Herb that is 15% THC, this is 1/2 teaspoon per serving). This technique works great with maple syrup (for brunch!), barbecue sauce, any kind of dipping sauce, ketchup, a wine pan sauce. You name it.

• ON A SALAD: Ask your guest to bring their salad with the dressing on the side, then stir the CannaOil into the dressing before tossing it with the salad.

• AS A DRIZZLE: For roasted vegetables, soup, chili . . . just drizzle 1/2 teaspoon (for 5 mg THC) of CannaOil or CannaButter (page 26) straight over the serving.

• AS A SPRINKLE: Have a mason jar with your decarbed Herb seasoning of choice (pages 45 to 49) ready for action and before serving sprinkle over guacamole, rice, couscous, mashed potatoes. . . anything really.

• IN A COMPOUND BUTTER: Beat decarbed Herb into a stick of softened butter (it needs to be well mixed so the herb is evenly dispersed). Add roasted garlic, shallots, citrus zest, or chopped Herbs, then roll the butter into a cylinder, chill, and serve over anything at all—even toast for brunch.

• FOR SWEETS: Make whipped cream to top just about *any* dessert and whip in CannaVanilla Extract (page 29).

IF YOU'RE JUST GETTING INTO SPIKING DISHES with Herb, this is a great beginner main dish to try out. Just enhance it, serve a salad on the side, and you're good to go. It's also excellent party food since it feeds eight, but that said, you can halve the recipe and make it in a 9-inch baking dish to serve four. Or, double up and stash one in the freezer so a party is always just a defrost away. This lasagna is decadent and cheesy but also loaded with vegetables: scallions, mushrooms, spinach, tomatoes, roasted peppers, and an entire *head* of garlic. Garlic is so good for you and packed with antioxidants that, in my opinion, you just can't eat too much of it (though my husband sometimes disagrees). You can use no-boil lasagna noodles if you like, in which case you will skip the first step.

MY VEG LASAGNA

16 lasagna noodles (a little less than a 1-pound box)

1 tablespoon plus 1¾ teaspoons fine sea salt

3 tablespoons plus 1 teaspoon extra-virgin olive oil

1 small head of garlic (about 8 medium cloves), minced

2 tablespoons finely chopped fresh thyme

½ teaspoon freshly ground black pepper

½ teaspoon chipotle chile powder or red pepper flakes

2 tablespoons tomato paste

½ cup finely chopped roasted red peppers

1 can (28 ounces) crushed tomatoes (preferably fire-roasted)

1 tablespoon plus 1 teaspoon CannaOil (page 25)

6 scallions, finely chopped

2 cups veggie crumbles or crumbled veggie burgers (thawed if frozen)

8 ounces button mushrooms, thinly sliced

3 cups baby spinach leaves

1½ cups fresh basil leaves, thinly sliced

1 pound fresh mozzarella cheese, shredded with your fingers into small pieces

2 cups grated young Gouda cheese (about 6 ounces)

1 cup finely grated Parmigiano-Reggiano cheese (about 3 ounces)

1. Bring a large pot of water to a boil. Add the lasagna noodles and 1 tablespoon of the salt and cook until al dente, according to the package directions. Drain and sprinkle with 1 teaspoon of the olive oil and set aside.

(recipe continues)

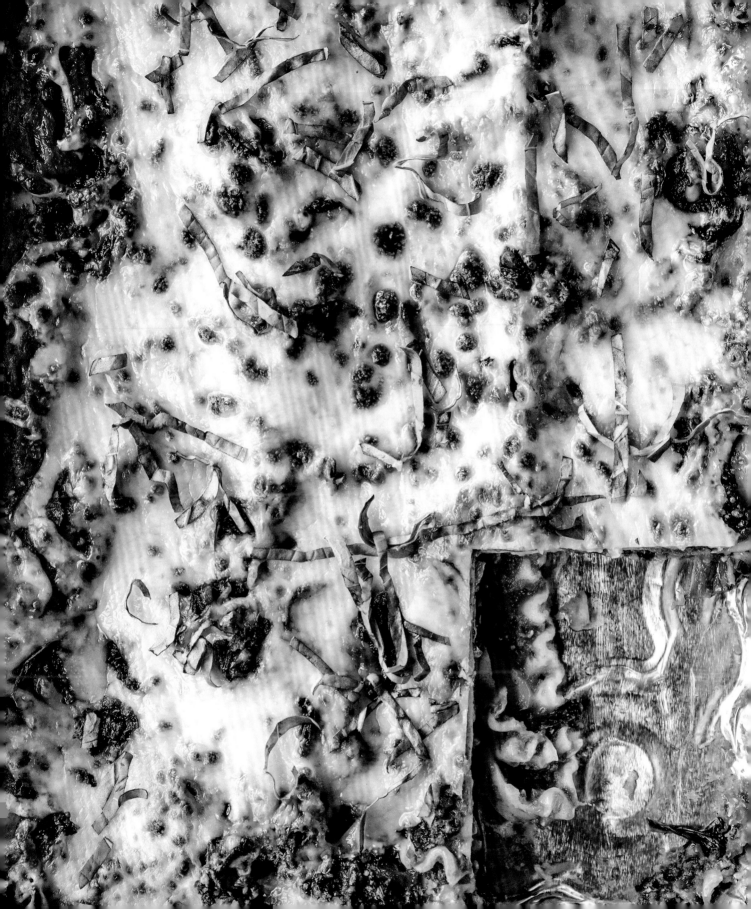

2. Heat 1 tablespoon of the olive oil in a large skillet. Add half of the garlic and the thyme and warm over medium heat until the garlic and herb are fragrant, about 30 seconds. Add the black pepper, chipotle powder, and the tomato paste and cook, stirring often, until the tomato paste darkens, 2 to 3 minutes. Stir in the roasted red peppers, then add the crushed tomatoes, CannaOil, and 1 teaspoon of the salt and cook, stirring occasionally, until the sauce becomes thick, 10 to 12 minutes (if your tomatoes are very chunky, use a potato masher to smash them so the sauce looks pasty rather than chunky). Transfer the sauce to a bowl.

3. Heat 1 tablespoon of the olive oil in another large skillet over medium-high heat. Add the scallions and cook until they start to brown, stirring occasionally, 2 to 3 minutes. Stir in the veggie crumbles and cook until they start to sizzle, about 1 minute. Stir in the mushrooms and the remaining 1 tablespoon oil and ¾ teaspoon salt and cook, stirring occasionally, scraping up any browned bits from the bottom of the pan, until the mushrooms soften, 5 to 6 minutes. Stir in the remaining garlic and cook until it is fragrant, about 30 seconds. Remove from the heat and stir in the spinach leaves and 1 cup of the basil and set aside.

4. Preheat the oven to 375°F.

5. Place the mozzarella in one bowl and mix the Gouda and Parmigiano together in another bowl. Place a few spoonfuls of sauce in the bottom of a 9 x 13-inch baking dish. Overlap 4 lasagna noodles across the bottom of the pan. Arrange a few more noodles around the sides of the pan. Add ¾ cup of the sauce to the pan followed by half of the veggie crumble mixture, one-third of the mozzarella, and one-third of the Gouda mixture. Add another pasta layer followed by more sauce, the rest of the veggie crumble mixture and half of the remaining mozzarella and Gouda mixture. Repeat one more time with the rest of the noodles, sauce, and cheese.

6. Bake the lasagna until it is golden brown on top and the sauce is bubbling, 35 to 40 minutes. Remove from the oven and serve sprinkled with the remaining ½ cup basil.

VARIATION: INDIVIDUAL LASAGNA WONTON CUPS

Sometimes I like to make individual lasagnas by lining each lightly greased cup of a muffin tin with 2 wonton wrappers, letting the edges poke up around the sides. Then I layer the lasagna fillings inside. The cheese somehow holds it all together and it's a fun and different way to serve appetizer-size lasagna (especially great for parties). Layer the vegetables and cheese with just a spoonful of the sauce so the wonton wrappers don't get too soggy and finish the mini lasagnas with grated cheese for the prettiest look. Start checking them about 18 minutes after they go into the oven.

I'M NOT EVEN GOING TO PRETEND that this macaroni and cheese is healthy—when you commit to making this, you've got to go *all in*! It's all about a luscious and creamy three-cheese sauce made with cheddar, Gruyère, and Parmigiano-Reggiano that gets finished with a crisp panko-parmesan bread crumb topping. It is *rich*, and is so, so good on a rainy or snowy day when all you want to do is chill out and watch movies with friends. For a large group of people, double the recipe and use a 9 x 13-inch baking dish. You can also make individual servings by using ramekins, which you then serve on a plate. So cute! At 5 milligrams THC per serving, seconds of this are totally cool (but you may want to think twice on thirds . . .).

ALL-IN MACARONI AND CHEESE

SERVES 6 (5 MG THC PER SERVING)

5 tablespoons unsalted butter, at room temperature

3 slices white bread, crusts removed

⅓ cup finely grated Parmigiano-Reggiano cheese

1¾ teaspoons fine sea salt, plus extra for cooking the pasta

½ pound elbow macaroni

¼ cup all-purpose flour

2 cups whole milk, warmed

½ teaspoon ground turmeric

¼ teaspoon ground allspice

¼ teaspoon cayenne pepper (optional)

¼ teaspoon garlic powder

¼ teaspoon freshly grated nutmeg

¼ teaspoon freshly ground black pepper

1 tablespoon CannaOil (page 25) or CannaButter (page 26)

1½ cups grated Gruyère cheese (6 ounces)

1 cup grated sharp cheddar cheese (4 ounces)

1. Preheat the oven to 375°F. Grease an 8-inch square baking dish or 2-quart casserole with 1 tablespoon of the butter.

2. Finely chop the bread to make bread crumbs (or pulse them in a food processor until fine) and place them in a medium bowl. Melt 1 tablespoon of the butter and pour over

the bread crumbs. Add half of the Parmigiano and ¼ teaspoon of the salt and toss to combine. Set aside.

3. Bring a large pot of water to a boil. Add the pasta and some salt and cook until al dente, according to the package directions. Drain and set aside.

4. Melt the remaining 3 tablespoons butter in a medium saucepan over medium heat. Whisk in the flour until it is smooth. Reduce the heat to medium-low and cook, whisking constantly, until the flour turns pale golden, about 2 minutes.

5. Whisk in the warm milk, a little at a time to avoid lumps (it will thicken with each addition), and once all the milk is added, continue to cook the mixture, whisking constantly, for 1 minute. Stir in the turmeric, allspice, cayenne (if using), garlic powder, nutmeg, remaining salt, and black pepper. Remove from the heat, stir in the CannaOil or CannaButter, and add the Gruyère, cheddar, and remaining Parmigiano. Use a wooden spoon to stir until the cheese is mostly melted, then stir in the cooked pasta.

6. Turn the mixture into the prepared pan. Sprinkle evenly with the bread crumb mixture. Bake until the bread crumbs are browned and the macaroni and cheese is bubbling, 25 to 30 minutes. Remove from the oven and serve immediately.

HERB + LIFE:
BREATHE IN POSITIVE

I'm a social creature and I love filling my home with friends and jumping on any excuse to make a ton of food, gather, and hang out. But I also really treasure these moments when I can relax, clear my mind, and re-center my spirit—and Herb is a wonderful way to help you settle in to that mellow vibe. It's important to be quiet and introspective now and then. Lots of people like to do yoga or meditate with Herb. Making an Herb-enhanced tea or smoothie or even a soulful spiked porridge in the morning puts you on that path to quietness and contemplation—be sure to use an indica-forward strain that is more conducive to chill moments rather than a sativa-dominant strain that is known for being more energizing.

When I take these moments for myself, which I do every single day, I hone in on positivity, and focus on ways to be the best me. I think I got this from my parents—Daddy and Mommy instilled within us kids an energy and resourcefulness and a sense of familial responsibility; they taught us that being positive and meditating on the good in life attracts positive people and uplifting circumstances. Herb is a great tool for getting there and letting go—it is more pure than pouring even a glass of wine. Do it in the morning or at the end of the day if evening is a better time for you to take a moment and zen out. It really doesn't matter when you do it, just do it—take the time to push out any negativity. Positivity and good things in life begin with you!

"Say you just can't live
that negative way,
if you know what I mean,
make way for that positive day."
—BOB MARLEY

MY MOTHER, RITA, loves her roti filled with chicken foot curry, and I like seitan or tofu. But honestly, this coconut-rich curry is delicious made with just about anything from calabaza squash to cauliflower, eggplant, or cabbage . . . or try it with goat like they make it in the Caribbean. Roti is a flatbread that we stuff with cooked yellow split peas. They are griddle-cooked until both sides are blistered a little and the roti is flaky and tender. Rip it up and dunk it in the curry—oh, is it good! The roti can be made and rolled a day ahead of cooking, then griddled the next day. Just wrap them well in plastic so they don't dry out.

||||||||||||||||||||||||||||||||||||||||||||||||||||||||||||||||||||||||||||||||||||||||||||||||||||||||||

CURRY WITH RITTY ROTI

|||||||||||||||||||||||||||||||||||| MAKES 8 ROTI (5 MG THC PER ROTI) ||||||||||||||||||||||||||||||||

ROTI

⅓ cup yellow split peas

1½ cups all-purpose flour, plus extra for rolling

1½ teaspoons baking powder

1½ teaspoons fine sea salt

½ teaspoon ground cumin

½ teaspoon ground ancho or chipotle chile (not the chili powder used to make chili)

¼ teaspoon ground turmeric

3 tablespoons chilled coconut oil (so it is solid)

8 tablespoons melted butter or ghee

CURRY

2 tablespoons coconut oil

1 tablespoon annatto seeds

1 medium yellow onion, quartered and thickly sliced crosswise

2 medium garlic cloves, finely chopped

1 Scotch bonnet pepper, finely chopped (seeded for less heat)

1 tablespoon Jamaican curry powder

1 tablespoon ground coriander

1 teaspoon sweet paprika

¼ teaspoon ground allspice

2 teaspoons fine sea salt

1 can (13.5 ounces) light coconut milk

2 tablespoons CannaOil (page 25)

8 ounces protein or hearty vegetables (such as seitan, tofu, eggplant, calabaza squash, cauliflower, boneless and skinless chicken thighs . . .), cut into bite-size pieces (about 2 cups)

3 medium red or purple potatoes (about ¾ pound), cut into 1-inch pieces

1 large red bell pepper, cut into 1-inch pieces

2 cups green peas (fresh or frozen)

Chopped fresh parsley (optional), for serving

(recipe continues)

1. **MAKE THE ROTI:** Bring a medium saucepan of water to a boil over high heat. Add the split peas, reduce the heat to medium-low, and gently simmer until the split peas are tender, about 30 minutes. Drain the split peas into a fine-mesh sieve. Set aside.

2. While the split peas are cooking, whisk together the flour, baking powder, salt, cumin, chile powder, and turmeric in a medium bowl. Add the solid coconut oil and work it in with your fingers until the dough is flaky. Make a well in the center of the flour mixture and add 6 tablespoons cool water. Start to work the ingredients together—after 30 seconds to 1 minute, you should be able to squeeze a small bit of dough and have it stick together without crumbling apart. If it is still too dry, add more water, 1 tablespoon at a time, until it holds together. Continue to knead the dough gently, pressing it against the sides of the bowl until it is soft and smooth, 1 to 2 minutes. Cover the dough with a damp paper towel and set aside to rest for 30 minutes.

3. **ROLL OUT THE ROTI DOUGH:** Place the dough on a floured work surface. Roll it back and forth to shape it into a log about 6 inches long, then cut it crosswise into 4 equal pieces. Flour the work surface again and use a rolling pin to roll one portion into an 8-inch round about 1/16 inch thick, reflouring the dough and work surface and flipping the dough over occasionally so it doesn't stick. Brush the dough with some of the melted butter (save the remainder for cooking the roti). Sprinkle 1/4 cup of the cooled split peas over the dough in an even layer and use your hands to press them into the dough. Use a paring knife to make a slit in the dough from the center of the round to an edge. Lift one side, tuck the cut edge under and roll the dough around to the other side so you end up with a cone shape that is narrow at the base and wide at the top.

4. Hold the cone in one hand and use your fingers to press the ragged ends into the middle of the cone, without pushing all the way through the cone (it will look something like a donut). Flip the cone over and repeat with the other side. You will end up with a fat donut-shaped piece of dough. Set the roti on a floured plate and cover with a damp paper towel. Repeat with the remaining pieces of dough and let them rest for 45 minutes.

5. **WHILE THE ROTI RESTS, MAKE THE CURRY:** Add the coconut oil and annatto seeds to a small saucepan set over medium heat. Infuse the oil, stirring often, until the oil is tinted red, 1 1/2 to 2 minutes, taking care not to let the seeds burn. Strain the oil through a fine-mesh sieve and into a large pot. Discard the seeds.

6. Set the pot over medium-high heat and add the onion, garlic, and Scotch bonnet, cooking until they soften, 3 to 4 minutes. Stir in the curry powder, coriander, paprika, allspice, and salt. Once the spices are fragrant, about 30 seconds, add the coconut

milk and ½ cup water. Bring the liquid to a boil over high heat, then reduce the heat to medium-low and add the CannaOil, protein or hearty vegetable, potatoes, and bell pepper. Cover the pot and simmer, stirring often so nothing sticks to the bottom, until the potatoes are tender, about 30 minutes. Taste and season with more salt if needed. Remove from the heat.

7. **FINISH THE ROTI:** Place the first piece of dough on a lightly floured work surface and slice it in half horizontally (so you have 2 circles). Flour the top of one piece and roll it into a very thin 6½- to 7-inch-diameter round. Repeat with the other pieces of dough to make 8 rolled roti.

8. Heat a medium nonstick skillet over medium heat. Use a silicone or pastry brush to lightly coat the pan with some melted butter. Set one rolled dough in the skillet, and cook until the top bubbles, 1 to 2 minutes. Brush the top with melted butter. Use a spatula to flip the roti over and brush the second side with melted butter. Cook until the bottom is golden with brown spots, 1½ to 2 minutes total. Flip and cook the other side until it has brown spots, then transfer the roti to a large plate and cover with a towel. Repeat with the remaining dough circles.

9. **FINISH THE CURRY:** Add the peas to the curry and warm the mixture over medium heat until the peas are warmed through, about 2 minutes. Serve the curry sprinkled with parsley and with the roti on the side.

NOTE You can skip the roti and serve the curry with Gungo Rice 'n Peas (page 185), spinners (page 173), or boiled green bananas (page 73) too, but you'd really be missing out.

TACOS KICK BUTT at a Super Bowl party or on game night, and because these are meatless just about everyone can enjoy them. The crumbly texture of my scrambled tofu kind of mimics the crumbly quality of ground meat and has tons of flavor from jerk paste and spices—that plus the mango and black bean salsa makes these tacos hit all the right notes. You could put a big bowl of the tofu out (be sure to add a note telling your guests that it is Herb enhanced) alongside a bowl of other fillings—maybe Hemp Guacamole (page 101), some corn, shredded grilled chicken (like leftover jerk chicken on page 141—so fantastic in a taco), jerk veggies (page 123), or fried fish (page 118). I like this salsa so much, I could wrap it in a tortilla with an avocado slice and eat it on its own—so sometimes I make a double batch of it and do just that.

JERK TOFU TACO WITH BLACK BEAN–MANGO SALSA

SERVES 4 (5 MG THC PER SERVING), WITH LEFTOVER SALSA

SALSA

1 cup finely chopped mango

1 cup cooked black beans

1 small red bell pepper, finely chopped

½ small red onion, very finely chopped

¼ cup finely chopped fresh basil, parsley, or cilantro leaves

Grated zest and juice of 1 lime

½ Scotch bonnet pepper or 1 medium jalapeño, finely chopped (seeded for less heat)

½ teaspoon fine sea salt

TACOS

1 package (14 ounces) firm tofu, drained

Unenhanced Jerk Paste (page 46)

1 tablespoon sweet paprika

½ teaspoon fine sea salt

1 tablespoon coconut oil

1 teaspoon ground cumin

1 teaspoon ground coriander

2 teaspoons CannaOil (page 25)

8 corn tortillas, warmed

1. **MAKE THE SALSA:** Stir together the mango, black beans, bell pepper, onion, basil, lime juice and zest, Scotch bonnet, and salt in a medium bowl. Set aside for the flavors to

(recipe continues)

come together, at least 30 minutes or up to a few hours (refrigerate if you're making more than 2 hours ahead of time; the salsa is best served within 1 day of making).

2. **MARINATE THE TOFU:** Line a colander or fine-mesh sieve with 2 paper towels. Crumble the tofu into the sieve, place 2 paper towels on top, and set a bowl on top—it should be small enough to press flush against the tofu but big enough to fill the diameter of the colander or sieve. Place something heavy in the bowl like a bag of dried beans or a can of tomatoes and set the colander in the sink to drain for 20 minutes. Turn the tofu out into a medium bowl, add the jerk paste, paprika, and salt, then use your hands to toss together. Marinate the tofu for at least 30 minutes or overnight in the refrigerator.

3. Heat a large skillet over high heat for 30 seconds. Reduce the heat to medium and add the coconut oil. Stir in the cumin and coriander and cook just 15 seconds, until the spices turn golden (this happens fast—don't walk away or the spices could burn!). Add the marinated tofu and stir to combine. Let the tofu brown without stirring for about 5 minutes, then continue to cook the tofu, stirring occasionally, until it starts to stick to the pan, about 5 minutes longer. Stir in the CannaOil, remove from the heat, and set aside.

4. Place 2 tortillas on each of 4 plates. Divide the jerk tofu among the tortillas. Top with some of the salsa and serve.

NOTE For a more steak-like effect, instead of crumbling and pan-frying the tofu, you can slice it into ½-inch-thick rectangles, brush it with a little oil, then grill or broil it. Baste often with lots of jerk paste until the tofu browns and firms up.

VEGGIE BURGERS ARE SO VERSATILE and you can shape them ahead and freeze them, making them the perfect option when it's late at night and you want to keep the party going without heading into the kitchen. Just bake them ahead of time and wrap them up, refrigerate or freeze them, then re-warm in the oven for a softer burger or in a skillet for a crisper one. These are loaded with vegetables, heat, spices, and so much good-for-you stuff like beans and flaxseeds.

ISLAND BEET BURGERS WITH AVOCADO AND JERK-FRIED ONIONS

MAKES 6 BURGERS (5 MG THC PER BURGER)

BURGERS

3 tablespoons flaxmeal

1 tablespoon neutral oil, plus a little extra for the baking sheet

1 small red onion, finely chopped

1 small green bell pepper, finely chopped

2 teaspoons ground cumin

¾ teaspoon chipotle chile powder

½ teaspoon fine sea salt

½ teaspoon freshly ground black pepper

¼ teaspoon cayenne pepper

3 medium garlic cloves, minced

1 small beet (about 4 ounces), peeled and halved

8 ounces seitan

1 cup panko bread crumbs

¾ cup cooked black beans

1 tablespoon soy sauce

1 tablespoon CannaOil (page 25)

JERK FRIED ONIONS

1 large red onion, sliced crosswise into ½-inch-thick rings

3 tablespoons plus 1 teaspoon neutral oil

2 teaspoons Jerk Seasoning (page 45)

¼ teaspoon kosher salt

2 tablespoons all-purpose flour

FOR SERVING

1 avocado, halved and pitted

½ teaspoon fine sea salt

1 tablespoon fresh lime juice

4 burger buns

(recipe continues)

1. **MAKE THE BURGERS:** Preheat the oven to 350°F. Line a rimmed baking sheet with foil.

2. Stir together the flaxmeal and 3 tablespoons cool water in a small bowl. Set aside.

3. Heat the oil in a medium nonstick skillet over medium-high heat. Add the onion, bell pepper, cumin, chipotle powder, salt, black pepper, and cayenne. Reduce the heat to medium and cook, stirring often, until the onion and pepper start to soften, about 3 minutes. Stir in the garlic and once it becomes fragrant, after about 30 seconds, remove from the heat and set the mixture aside.

4. In a food processor fitted with the shredder disk, grate the beet (or grate it on the medium holes of a box grater). Leave the beets in the processor and switch to the metal blade. Add the onion-pepper mixture along with the seitan, panko, black beans, soy sauce, and CannaOil. Add the flaxseed mixture (it should be thick like a gel) and pulse until the mixture is semismooth with some texture, about six 1-second pulses.

5. Grease the foil-lined baking sheet with a little oil. Use your oiled hands to pack some of the beet mixture into a ½-cup measuring cup. Turn it out onto the baking sheet and gently flatten the mixture into a 3½- to 4-inch wide and ½-inch-thick patty. Repeat with the rest of the mixture. Bake the burgers until they feel crisp and dry and resist light pressure, turning them midway through cooking, about 25 minutes total.

6. **MEANWHILE, MAKE THE JERK ONIONS:** Place the onion rings in a medium bowl and drizzle with 1 teaspoon of the oil, then toss with the jerk seasoning and salt. Add the flour and toss to combine. Pour the remaining 3 tablespoons oil into a large skillet, set over medium-high heat, and heat the oil until you see ripples in it, 1 to 2 minutes. Fry the onions until they are browned on all sides, using a fork or chopsticks to turn the onion rings often, about 4 minutes total. Transfer the fried onions to a plate lined with paper towels.

7. **WHEN READY TO SERVE:** Place the avocado in a small bowl and smash with the salt and lime juice. Toast the burger buns cut-side down on a grill pan or cut-side up under the broiler. Spread the top halves of the buns with the avocado. Set a burger on each bottom half and top with the fried onions. Place the burger bun on top and serve.

NOTE For a burger bar, have all of the patties on a bun bottom, then line up a whole bunch of toppings—you could include salsa, hummus, honey mustard, hot sauce, Guava Ketchup (page 114), all kinds of veggies or even pickled veggies (page 116), . . . so good!

FLAVOR:
TERROIR AND TERPENES

If you like wine (and I do like wine!), chances are you have heard the word "terroir." Terroir refers to how the land on which the grapes are grown affects the wine. Stony soil and a northern climate will likely produce a more mineral-y drier wine, while soil rich in volcanic ash and blessed with sunshine and warm weather will produce bolder, fruitier wines. Terroir can also effect Herb. For example, Herb grown in the "Emerald Triangle" in Northern California (Mendocino, Humboldt, and Trinity counties) is exposed to sun, fog, and rugged terrain. The Herb grown there benefits from the natural mineral profiles in the soil, which are compounded into a unique expression of flavor. Herb grown in the Emerald Triangle will taste and express itself totally differently from the same strain grown under artificial lights in a grow house.

Another major factor when it comes to flavor are terpenes. Terpenes exist in the essential oils of plants and fruits. Take lemons, rosemary, and lavender for example. The unique fragrance and taste that is associated with each of those ingredients is caused by the terpene found in the plant. Herb has terpenes as well—they are what give Pineapple Kush its tropical-sweet-floral vibe or Lemon Haze is citrusy fresh flavor. Here is a list of common terpenes found in Herb and how they can influence your experience.

ALSO FOUND IN	FLAVOR/S	TERPENE	EFFECT
Black Pepper, Cloves	Spicy, Earthy	Caryophyllene	Anti-inflammatory
Lavender	Floral, Sweet	Linalool	Anxiety Relief
Rosemary, Basil	Pine	Pinene	Alertness, Creativity
Lemongrass, Thyme, Hops	Musky, Citrus	Myrcene	Relaxation, Sleepiness
Grapefruit, Orange	Citrus	Limonene	Stress Relief

ITAL STEW IS KIND OF LIKE JAMAICAN CHILI, but instead of cornbread or tortilla chips, we add dumplings, called spinners, to the pot. The word "Ital" comes from the word "vital," tapping into the idea of the essential life force and goodness that Rastafarians embrace and put out into the world. This very healthy stew is extra hearty thanks to squash, potatoes, and red kidney beans (which we call red peas, see page 185). To speed things up, yes, you could use canned beans instead of starting with dried, but the texture of fresh cooked beans is really unmatched—you should try it at least once. Spinners are little flour dumplings made by taking a small piece of dough and rubbing it between your palms, "spinning" it if you will, into a long twisty cylinder. They are cooked directly in the stew and soak up all that good flavor. Sometimes I like to use half whole wheat flour or all white whole wheat flour for the extra fiber and nutrition for spinners, but the dumplings will be more stick-to-your-ribs! (You may need to add a little extra water since whole wheat flour will absorb more liquid.)

ITAL STEW WITH SPINNERS

SERVES 6 (5 mg THC per serving)

BEANS

1 cup dried kidney beans

Vegetable broth or water

7 allspice berries

4 medium garlic cloves, roughly chopped

2-inch piece fresh ginger, peeled

1½ cups light coconut milk

SPINNERS

¾ cup all-purpose flour

¼ teaspoon fine sea salt

STEW

2 cups peeled or unpeeled calabaza, Hubbard, kabocha, or butternut squash pieces (¾ inch)

1 large red potato, peeled and cut into ¾-inch pieces

2 medium carrots, peeled and cut crosswise at an angle into ½-inch-thick slices

2 teaspoons fine sea salt

1 tablespoon CannaOil (page 25)

8 fresh thyme sprigs

2 ripe plantains, peeled and cut crosswise at an angle into ½-inch-thick slices

1 Scotch bonnet pepper, pricked a few times with a fork

2 whole scallions, thinly sliced

(recipe continues)

1. **SOAK AND COOK THE BEANS:** Add the beans to a soup pot and add enough cold water to cover them by 1½ inches. Set aside to soak overnight. The next morning, add enough vegetable broth to again cover the beans by 1½ inches. Add the allspice and garlic to the beans. Halve the ginger lengthwise and use the flat side of a chef's knife to smash it, then add it to the pot. Bring the water to a boil over high heat, reduce the heat to a gentle simmer, and cook the beans until they are nearly tender, about 40 minutes. Add the coconut milk and continue to cook, stirring occasionally, for 20 minutes.

2. **MAKE THE STEW:** Add the squash, potato, carrot, and salt to the beans. Increase the heat to high and bring to a boil, then reduce the heat to medium-low and cook, stirring often for 8 minutes.

3. While the stew simmers, make the spinners: Combine the flour and salt in a medium bowl. Use a fork to stir in ¼ cup room-temperature water. Mix and knead the dough until it is smooth and it holds together without crumbling apart (you may need to add another 1 to 2 tablespoons water), 1 to 2 minutes. Break off a grape-size piece of dough and roll it between your palms to make a 1½-inch-long rope. Drop the rope into the stew. Repeat with the remaining dough—you should get about 32 spinners. Stir the spinners occasionally until they float to the surface, 5 to 8 minutes. By now the vegetables should be tender.

4. Add the CannaOil, thyme, plantains, and Scotch bonnet to the stew. Continue to cook until the plantain is tender, 20 to 30 minutes longer.

5. Remove from the heat and pull out the ginger pieces, the herb sprigs, and allspice berries (if you can find them!). Serve sprinkled with scallions.

ONE-POT IS LIKE THE JAMAICAN ANSWER TO A CASSEROLE, with everything cooked together, as the name suggests, in one pot. The most traditional version is made with saltfish, a salt-preserved whitefish, usually cod, hake, or pollack. It's often sold in the seafood section of the grocery store, sometimes in an open box where you can pick your own, sometimes prepackaged in a sealed bag. Saltfish can have a very intense flavor, and if you're not a fan, just leave it out for a perfectly tasty vegetarian version. If you can't find calabaza squash, you can use unpeeled acorn squash instead.

SALTFISH ONE-POT

SERVES 6 (5 mg THC per serving)

½ pound saltfish (salt cod)

2 tablespoons coconut oil

1 tablespoon annatto seeds

2-inch piece fresh ginger, peeled and grated

2 tablespoons curry powder

6 whole scallions, finely chopped

1 medium yellow onion, finely chopped

1 Scotch bonnet pepper, finely chopped

½ pound calabaza squash, seeded and chopped (no need to peel) into bite-size pieces (about 1½ cups)

1 teaspoon fine sea salt

1 tablespoon unsalted butter

1 tablespoon CannaButter (page 26)

1½ cups white basmati rice

1 can (14 ounces) coconut milk

1 fresh thyme sprig

Hot sauce (optional), preferably one made with Scotch bonnet

1. Bring a large pot of water to a boil. Add the saltfish, reduce the heat to medium, set a cover halfway on the pot, and "scald" the fish at a gentle simmer for 20 minutes. Drain the fish, dry it between paper towels, pressing firmly to extract as much water as possible. Remove the skin and bones (if there are any) and finely chop the cod into small bits.

2. Melt the coconut oil in a large pot over medium heat. Add the annatto seeds and cook, stirring often, until they tint the oil yellow and start to sizzle, 1½ to 2 minutes. Drain the oil through a fine-mesh sieve, discard the seeds, and return the annatto oil to the pot.

3. Add the ginger and curry powder to the oil and cook, stirring often, until the ginger becomes dry, 3 to 4 minutes. Stir in half of the scallions, the onion, Scotch bonnet, squash, and salt and cook, stirring often, until the onion becomes golden, about 5 minutes. Pour in 1 cup water, bring to a boil over high heat, reduce the heat to medium, and simmer, stirring occasionally, until the mixture becomes thick and the squash softens around the edges, about 10 minutes.

4. Increase the heat to medium-high and stir in the butter and CannaButter. Once the butter is melted, stir in the rice, coconut milk, and 1 cup water. Bring the liquid a boil, reduce the heat to medium, stir in the saltfish, and gently simmer, stirring occasionally (the rice has a tendency to stick to the bottom), until the mixture is very creamy and the rice is about halfway cooked through, about 10 minutes. Place the thyme sprigs on top of the rice, cover the pot, reduce the heat to low, and cook until the rice is tender, about 10 minutes longer. Remove from the heat and let the rice stand, covered, for 5 minutes. Discard the thyme and serve sprinkled with the remaining scallions, with hot sauce on the side.

SOUP IS A GREAT WAY TO BRING HERB INTO A MEAL. Since it is usually served as the first course, it will bring the feeling of fineness on in a mellow way so that by the time dessert is served, you're feeling quite nice. This soup is loaded with all kinds of vegetables from yam to bell peppers and a full pound of spinach that gives the soup broth its creamy green color. Traditionally in Jamaica the soup is made with callaloo (page 104), but spinach is an absolutely fine substitute (Swiss chard works too). Jamaican yellow yams (page 39) are quite starchy and need to be peeled and handled with care—I wear gloves—as the juices from the yam can cause your hands to itch like crazy. If you don't have access to a Caribbean market to buy yellow yams, substitute a Japanese sweet potato instead. These are maroon-skinned white sweet potatoes that are starchy and a little sweet, but not as sweet as the American sweet potatoes that come from the South.

PEPPERPOT SOUP

SERVES 8 (5 MG THC PER SERVING)

2 tablespoons coconut oil

6 scallions, white and light green parts only, thinly sliced

2 medium carrots, peeled and finely chopped

1 red bell pepper, finely chopped

1 teaspoon fine sea salt

1 teaspoon freshly ground black pepper

2 teaspoons finely chopped fresh thyme leaves

5 cups vegetable broth, homemade (page 180) or store-bought

1¼ pounds Jamaican yellow yams or Japanese sweet potatoes, peeled and chopped into bite-size pieces

1 Scotch bonnet pepper, pricked a few times with a fork

1 pound spinach, root ends trimmed

1 cup coconut milk

1 tablespoon plus 1 teaspoon CannaOil (page 25)

12 okra pods, stemmed and sliced crosswise into ¼-inch-thick rounds

I. Heat the oil in a large pot over medium heat. Add the scallions, carrots, bell pepper, salt, and black pepper and cook, stirring often, until the vegetables start to soften, about 5 minutes.

(recipe continues)

2. Stir in the thyme. Add 3 cups of the vegetable broth and bring the liquid to a boil over high heat. Reduce the heat to a gentle simmer and add the yams and Scotch bonnet and cook until the yam is about halfway tender, 12 to 15 minutes.

3. Meanwhile, heat the remaining 2 cups broth in a medium saucepan over medium-high heat. Once the broth is simmering, add a handful of the spinach. Once the spinach wilts, add another handful. Continue to add the spinach, stirring after each addition, until all of the spinach is added and wilted. Transfer the spinach and broth to a blender and puree until mostly smooth (some small pieces are nice and add texture).

4. Pour the spinach mixture into the soup pot. Add the coconut milk and CannaOil and gently simmer for 5 minutes. Add the okra and cook until it is tender, 2 to 3 minutes. Remove and discard the Scotch bonnet before serving.

HOMEMADE CARIBBEAN-STYLE VEGETABLE BROTH

|||||||||||||||||||||||||||||||||||||||||||| MAKES ABOUT 1½ QUARTS ||||||||||||||||||||||||||||||||||||||||||||

2 tablespoons neutral oil or coconut oil

1 large yellow onion, roughly chopped

2 medium carrots, peeled and roughly chopped

1 green bell pepper, chopped

6 scallions, white and light green parts only, coarsely chopped

4 garlic cloves, smashed

12 allspice berries

1 teaspoon black peppercorns

5 fresh parsley sprigs

5 fresh thyme sprigs

2 bay leaves

1 teaspoon fine sea salt

1. Heat the oil in a large pot over medium-high heat. Add the onion and carrots, reduce the heat to medium, and cook, stirring often, until they begin to soften, about 3 minutes.

2. Stir in the bell pepper, scallions, garlic, allspice berries, and peppercorns. Once the garlic is fragrant, after about 1 minute, add the parsley, thyme, bay leaves, and salt. Add 10 cups water, increase the heat to high, and bring the liquid to a boil. Reduce the heat to medium-low and gently simmer, stirring occasionally, for 1 hour.

3. Cool the broth for 20 minutes before straining through a fine-mesh sieve and into a large bowl or container (you should have 6 to 7 cups of broth). Refrigerate for up to 1 week or freeze in a quart or gallon-size resealable freezer bag.

A BIG "JAM DOWN" PARTY SPREAD would definitely include jerk chicken and absolutely potato salad. Consider dividing the salad in half and spiking one bowl; just be sure to label which is which!

ISLAND POTATO SALAD

SERVES 8 (5 MG THC PER SERVING)

4 medium Yukon Gold potatoes, peeled and cut into ¾-inch cubes

4 large cage-free eggs

1 tablespoon plus 1¼ teaspoons fine sea salt

1 cup green peas, fresh or frozen

2 tablespoons coconut oil

1 tablespoon annatto seeds

½ small red onion, very finely chopped

1 tablespoon Jamaican curry powder

1 teaspoon mustard powder

½ cup olive oil–based mayonnaise

1 tablespoon plus 1 teaspoon CannaOil (page 25)

6 whole scallions, finely chopped

1 Scotch bonnet pepper, seeded and minced

½ teaspoon sweet paprika

1. Bring a large pot of water to a boil. Add the potatoes, eggs, and 1 tablespoon of the salt and return to a boil. Simmer until the potatoes are nearly tender, 5 to 7 minutes. Add the peas and cook 1 minute, then drain in a colander. Peel the eggs and set aside.

2. Heat the coconut oil and annatto seeds in a small skillet over medium heat. Once the seeds sizzle and the oil turns a rich orange, 1½ to 2 minutes, strain the oil through a fine-mesh sieve into a bowl. Discard the seeds and return the oil to the skillet. Add the onion and ¼ teaspoon of the salt and cook over medium heat until it starts to sizzle. Stir in the curry powder and cook the mixture down until the curry powder is fragrant, about 1 minute. Transfer to a bowl and stir in the mustard powder.

3. Chop 2 of the peeled eggs, place them in a large bowl, and use a fork to mash them into bits. Stir in the mayonnaise, CannaOil, 1 teaspoon salt, the scallions, and Scotch bonnet, then stir in the cooled onion mixture. Stir in the potatoes and peas, then taste for salt.

4. Transfer to a serving bowl. Cut the remaining eggs into quarters and set them on top of the potato salad, sprinkle with paprika, and serve.

THIS SWEET, CREAMY, rich corn dish is a party favorite at my house. It brings a more sophisticated and refined quality to an Herb party—serve it with a kale salad (page 126) and maybe the Snapper Escovitch (page 139) or a piece of grilled jerk chicken (page 141) and you have a fine meal that could be served in any restaurant (but yours is better because it is made with love . . . and Herb!).

TRIPLE-THREAT
SPICY CORN BAKE

SERVES 8 (5 MG THC PER SERVING)

4 ears corn, shucked

1 cage-free egg, lightly beaten

2 cups whole milk, warmed

⅓ cup fine yellow cornmeal

3 tablespoons cane sugar

⅛ teaspoon cayenne pepper

1½ cups grated mild cheddar cheese

1½ teaspoons fine sea salt

1½ tablespoons unsalted butter, plus 1 tablespoon at room temperature

1 tablespoon plus 1 teaspoon CannaButter (page 26)

6 scallions, minced

2 jalapeño peppers, minced

1 Scotch bonnet pepper, minced

1 teaspoon chopped fresh thyme leaves

½ teaspoon freshly ground black pepper

¼ cup all-purpose flour

3 tablespoons chopped fresh flat-leaf parsley

1. Preheat the oven to 350°F.

2. Grate three ears of corn on the medium holes of a box grater into a large bowl. Hold the remaining ear of corn upright and use a large sharp knife to slice from top to bottom, removing the kernels from the cob. Add the kernels to the corn pulp. Whisk in the egg, then add 1 cup of the milk, the cornmeal, sugar, cayenne, ½ cup of the cheddar, and 1 teaspoon of the salt. Set aside.

(recipe continues)

3. Heat 1½ tablespoons of the butter and the CannaButter in a medium skillet over medium heat. Reduce the heat to medium and add the scallions, jalapeños, Scotch bonnet, thyme, ½ teaspoon of the salt, and the black pepper. Cook, stirring often, until the scallions are soft, about 2 minutes.

4. Stir the flour into the skillet and cook, stirring constantly, until it becomes golden, about 2 minutes. Gradually add the remaining 1 cup milk, stirring occasionally, so you don't get any lumps, then remove from the heat. Add the mixture to the corn mixture, whisking to combine.

5. Grease a 10-inch cast-iron skillet or a 1½-quart baking dish with the 1 tablespoon softened butter. Scrape in the corn mixture and bake for 30 minutes. Sprinkle with the remaining 1 cup cheddar and continue to bake until the edges are set and the center is just barely set (but a cake tester inserted into the center comes out clean), about 45 minutes. Remove from the oven, sprinkle with parsley, and serve.

LOVE THE DUTCHIE

Growing up, we didn't have all the fancy cookware you can get today. No triple-ply copper-core nonstick business. We had cast iron, plain and simple. Cooking in cast iron is actually smart because your food takes up some of the iron content from the pan and the pans last for decades and decades, even getting better and more seasoned—almost like a nonstick surface—with age if you care for them properly. Our dutchies (Dutch ovens) and frying pans were well seasoned from years and years of use. If you're not lucky enough to inherit a perfectly seasoned pot from a grandma or auntie, you can buy a new one inexpensively. Just season it well before you start cooking by coating with a nice thick layer of coconut oil and then placing it upside-down in a 350°F oven for 1 hour (put a piece of foil under the pan to catch drips). Turn off the oven and let it cool right in there, then it's good to go. It's best to clean a cast-iron pan while it's still hot. Use a stiff-bristled brush, kosher salt, and plenty of hot water to give it a good scrub-down. If food starts to stick, it's time to re-season!

IN JAMAICA you're likely to find and eat certain kinds of food on specific days of the week. Friday means curry and roti, and fried chicken with rice and peas is the dish of the day on Wednesdays. If you are looking for a way to put a little fun in your hump day, look no further than this simple, earthy dish. Gungo peas, as they're called in Jamaica, are also known as pigeon peas (or *gandules* in Latin markets). They are small, round, and tender and even people who say they don't love beans usually like gungo peas. Definitely take the time to make the gungo peas from scratch, starting with the dried beans. If you don't have the time, substitute canned kidney beans instead (see Variation on page 186), since canned kidney beans—which we call red peas!—hold up better than canned pigeon peas.

GUNGO RICE 'N PEAS

SERVES 8 (5 MG THC PER SERVING)

¾ cup dried pigeon peas (gandules)

2 tablespoons coconut oil

1 small white onion, finely chopped

2 teaspoons Garlic Salt (page 49)

1 scallion, ends trimmed

2 teaspoons finely chopped fresh thyme leaves

1-inch piece fresh ginger, peeled and finely chopped

1½ cups long-grain white rice

¾ cup coconut milk

1 tablespoon plus 1 teaspoon CannaOil (page 25)

1 Scotch bonnet pepper, pricked a few times with a fork

Fine sea salt, if needed

1. Place the pigeon peas in a medium bowl and add water to cover by a few inches. Soak the pigeon peas at room temperature overnight. The next day, drain the pigeon peas.

2. Heat the coconut oil in a medium pot over medium heat. Add the onion and Garlic Salt and cook, stirring often, until the onion is soft and translucent, 3 to 4 minutes. Stir in the drained peas and add enough water just to cover the peas by ½ inch. Bring the water to a boil, then reduce the heat to medium-low and gently simmer until the peas are tender, adding more water if the pan becomes dry, about 40 minutes (if the peas are old, they could take up to 1 hour).

(recipe continues)

3. Stir in the scallion, thyme and ginger, then stir in the rice. Add the coconut milk and CannaOil, give the rice a stir, then add enough water to cover the rice and peas by 1 inch. Add the Scotch bonnet and bring the liquid to a boil over high heat, reduce the heat to low, cover the pot, and gently cook the rice until the liquid is absorbed and the rice is tender, 14 to 16 minutes. Remove from the heat and let the rice stand, covered, for 10 minutes before removing and discarding the Scotch bonnet and the scallion, fluffing the peas and rice with a fork. Season with salt if needed and serve.

VARIATION: RICE 'N RED PEAS

Omit step 1. In step 2, fry the onion and Garlic Salt in the coconut oil as described, then skip to step 3. Add the scallion, thyme, and ginger and once the ginger is fragrant, stir in the rice, coconut milk, CannaOil, salt, and 1 can (14 or 15 ounces) of drained and rinsed red peas (kidney beans). Add enough water to cover the rice and beans by 1 inch. Proceed with the recipe as above.

JAMAICAN GUNGO PEAS

In Jamaica, we call pigeon peas gungo peas (just as we call kidney beans "red peas") but despite the nickname, they really are beans. Gungo peas are native to India, where they are boiled to make dal, the golden yellow soup. From India they traveled to Africa and Asia and are common in Central America as well, probably brought by slaves from their home country to wherever they landed. Some of them certainly ended up in Jamaica, where gungo peas are an island staple. When fresh, they're a great treat even when raw. Just pick a pod right off the bush, pop it open, and eat the green peas straight up! If you don't have your own bush, though, you're probably cooking dried peas. When dried they become hard like a small navy bean, and pale brown in color. Because they are small, they aren't mealy like bigger beans can be, making them a great alternative to navy beans or even black beans. In Jamaica we generally cook them with rice (page 185) or turn them into pea soup. Rice 'n peas is a must-have dish on any Jamaican Sunday table as well as at Christmas time.

6

SWEETS THAT SATISFY

"'Cause just like a tree planted,
planted by the rivers of water/
That bringeth forth fruits, bringeth
forth fruits in due season/
Everything in life got its
purpose, find its reason in
every season, forever!"

— "FOREVER LOVING JAH," BOB MARLEY

o into a dispensary to buy some edibles and what do you find? Gummies, chocolate truffles, Rice Krispies Treats, chocolate chip cookies . . . it's all sweets! If you have bought an Herb-enhanced edible, it probably has been in the form of dessert (think pot brownies, people). Maybe this is because long ago Herb wasn't as fresh and good as it is today, and covering its flavor with sugar, butter, and chocolate was the only way to make it taste okay. Or they're just more fun to eat than salad (not in my opinion, but I guess I can see this as being a general consensus). Luckily, the Herb you can buy now (or grow if you have seeds) is being farmed using more sustainable methods and is grown organically without chemicals and pesticides, so the Herb just has better flavor. It not only makes your main dish dinner taste *irie*, but also is great for your ice cream and carrot cake too. Baked sweets weren't a big part of my childhood—in fact, when we lived in Trenchtown, we didn't have enough money to own an oven. Needless to say, on special occasions we went to bakeries to satisfy our deep down sweet cravings. When I got older, though, we finally acquired an oven (yes!) and we started baking on the weekends—maybe a sweet potato pudding (page 199) or a carrot cake (page 197). Now I love to bake, and find it the perfect way to introduce the uninitiated into the pleasures of Herb-boosted foods for snacking or indulging throughout the day.

For a dinner party, though, you really want to think hard if you're going to enhance the sweets. Remember that it can take a bit of time for the Herb to kick in . . . so if you're serving dessert at nine o'clock at night, your guests might not feel the Herb until sometime between nine-thirty and eleven o'clock . . . it will make for a late (but fun, true) night. Take that into consideration when hosting a dinner party boosted with Herb infusions or spices, otherwise your dinner party might turn into a sleepover.

Also, while CannaButter and CannaOil can certainly be used to enhance sweets, if you're really thinking you want to get baked from your baking, consider investing the time to make CannaVanilla Extract (page 29). It needs to steep for a few weeks, but once it's ready to go you can use it in place of vanilla extract in any recipe you want to give a boost to. It's super shelf stable too, so make a few bottles and stash some and give away others as gifts! A little goes a long way, so you'll be feeling fine for a good long while.

I GUESS YOU COULD CALL MY PARENTS some of the original health nuts—we never had much in the way of sugary foods in our house, and dessert was something special, not an everyday kind of thing. (According to my dad, a raw carrot was dessert!) So when we were given a cookie or something sweet, it was a *big deal.* That said, Daddy loved to treat us kids, especially if we had a hard day or were upset or sad—off we'd go to the Oop Si Do ice cream parlor for a scoop of dragon stout, rum cake, Irish moss, soursop, sorrel, or my favorite, Grape-Nut. Here I enhance the ice cream with some CannaButter, which works great in the ice cream since you are making a custard base first to warm and distribute it. You can also use 1 teaspoon of CannaVanilla in place of the vanilla bean (and omit the CannaButter).

RUM RAISIN AND GRAPE-NUTS
ICE CREAM

SERVES 4 (MAKES 1 PINT; 5 MG THC PER SERVING)

3 cups half-and-half

1 vanilla bean, split lengthwise

5 large cage-free egg yolks

¾ cup cane sugar

2 teaspoons CannaButter (page 26) or CannaOil (page 25; preferably made with coconut oil)

¼ cup dark rum (preferably Jamaican rum)

½ cup raisins

1 cup Grape-Nuts cereal

1. Bring the half-and-half to a simmer in a saucepan over medium-high heat. Use the tip of a paring knife to scrape the vanilla seeds into the pot. Remove from the heat, cover, and set aside to steep for 30 minutes.

2. Whisk the egg yolks and sugar in a medium bowl. Remove the vanilla pod from the cream and discard. Return the cream to a simmer. While whisking, drizzle in a little of the hot cream into the yolks. Add another splash, whisk, and repeat until all of the cream is whisked in. Return the mixture to the saucepan and use a wooden spoon to stir it gently over medium heat, making sure to get into the corners of the pan, until slightly

(recipe continues)

thickened, 8 to 10 minutes. You should be able to draw a line through the custard on the back of the spoon.

3. Remove from the heat and pour the custard through a fine-mesh sieve into a medium bowl. Whisk in the CannaButter or CannaOil, then chill the custard in the refrigerator until completely cold, about 2 hours (or overnight), stirring every 30 minutes or so (cover the bowl with plastic after the first 30 minutes).

4. Warm the rum in a small saucepan just until it is warmed but not simmering, 30 seconds to 1 minute. Add the raisins, remove from the heat, cover, and set aside to plump.

5. Transfer the custard to an ice cream maker and freeze according to the manufacturer's instructions. When the ice cream is just about done churning, add the raisins with any leftover rum and the Grape-Nuts. Churn 1 minute longer, then transfer the ice cream to an airtight container and freeze for at least 3 hours before serving.

FAST AND EASY ENHANCED ICE CREAM

If you have a batch of CannaButter or CannaOil or CannaVanilla already made, you can have an enhanced ice cream dessert in no time. Here are some ways to spike your sweets by adding ½ teaspoon of CannaButter or CannaOil per serving (or ⅛ teaspoon CannaVanilla per serving).

• Add to store-bought chocolate sauce or dulce de leche to make an ice cream sundae

• Stir into store-bought ice cream with other add-ins like chocolate candies, fruit sauces, pretzels or broken up cookies

• Beat in with sugar to make sweetened whipped cream (that, along with a cherry on top, goes with any ice cream dessert from a banana split to a sundae or milkshake)

• Blend with milk and ice cream for a shake or malted

• Add Coconut CannaOil to melted chocolate for a hard-shell dip for ice cream (follow the instructions on page 208 for dipping brownies but dip frozen scoops of ice cream instead)

THIS IS A REALLY REFRESHING WAY to serve dessert or get your sweet fix almost any time of day. Because it's so light and refreshing, you could definitely get away with serving the sorbet and its psychedelically vibrant fuchsia-tinted raspberry sauce at a brunch or ladies' luncheon. The sauce, by the way, is good on virtually any kind of ice cream, from vanilla to chocolate (or even Grape-Nut, page 191), if you want to skip the sorbet and just serve the Herb-spiked sauce over a store-bought scoop.

CITRUS-GINGER SORBET WITH RAISE-UP RASPBERRY SAUCE

SERVES 4 (5 MG THC PER SERVING)

SORBET

2 cups demerara sugar

⅓ cup grated fresh ginger
(from about a 4-inch piece)

2 lemons

1 lime

RASPBERRY SAUCE

½ cup sugar

2 cups strawberries, hulled and halved
(set aside a few for serving)

2 cups raspberries (set aside a few
for serving)

Juice of ½ lemon

Pinch of fine sea salt

2 tablespoons unsalted butter

2 teaspoons CannaButter (page 26)

I. **MAKE THE SORBET:** Combine the sugar, ginger, and 5 cups water in a medium saucepan. Bring to a boil over high heat. Reduce the heat to medium-low and simmer gently, stirring often, until the sugar is dissolved and the syrup is slightly thick, about 10 minutes.

2. Set a fine-mesh sieve over a medium bowl and strain the sugar syrup, pressing on the grated ginger with a rubber spatula to extract all of the liquid. Discard the solids.

3. Grate the zest of 1 of the lemons and the lime, then juice both lemons and the lime. Add the zest and juice to the ginger syrup and refrigerate until the syrup is completely chilled.

4. Pour the chilled syrup into an ice cream maker and freeze according to the manufacturer's instructions. Transfer to an airtight container and freeze for at least 2 hours before serving.

5. **WHILE THE SORBET CHILLS, MAKE THE SAUCE:** Combine the sugar and ¼ cup water in a medium saucepan and bring to a simmer over medium-high heat, stirring occasionally, until the sugar is dissolved, about 2 minutes. Add the strawberries and raspberries, lemon juice, and salt. Once the liquid starts to bubble, remove from the heat.

6. Strain the sauce through a fine-mesh sieve into a clean bowl pressing on the liquid to get all of the juices through (discard the seeds). Return the sauce to the saucepan and set it over medium heat. Add the unsalted butter and CannaButter and stir until it is incorporated. Cool to room temperature, then serve over the sorbet. (The sauce can be made up to 1 week ahead of time; if the butter solidifies in the sauce, warm it in a saucepan until the consistency is smooth.)

7. Divide the sorbet among 4 bowls. Divide the sauce evenly over the servings and garnish with a few berries.

IF YOU'RE LOOKING TO MAKE A SPECIAL OCCASION even more special, a showstopper cake like this one with an extra secret ingredient is just what you need. Cake is really easy to enhance with Herb—just replace some of the butter or oil in the recipe with CannaButter or CannaOil and you're good to go. Cashews and crystallized ginger give the cake extra richness and a bit of sweet heat. The middle layer gets a special addition of pineapple in the cream cheese frosting. I like how it breaks up the layers and adds a touch of sweet-sour to the cake.

GINGERY CARROT CAKE WITH PINEAPPLE AND CASHEWS

SERVES 12 (MAKES ONE 9-INCH LAYER CAKE; 5 MG THC PER SERVING)

2½ cups all-purpose flour

2½ teaspoons baking powder

½ teaspoon baking soda

1½ tablespoons ground cinnamon

2 teaspoons ground allspice

2 teaspoons ground ginger

½ teaspoon fine sea salt

3 large cage-free eggs

1¾ cups packed dark brown sugar

6 medium carrots (12 ounces), peeled and grated (about 2 cups)

1 cup finely chopped roasted cashews

½ cup finely chopped crystallized ginger

⅔ cup pineapple juice (from one drained 8-ounce can crushed pineapple; save the pineapple for the frosting)

2 teaspoons vanilla extract

½ cup plus 2 tablespoons coconut oil

2 tablespoons CannaOil (page 25) or CannaButter (page 26)

FROSTING

2¼ sticks (9 ounces) unsalted butter, at room temperature

1¼ pounds (two 8-ounce bricks plus 2 tablespoons) cream cheese, at room temperature

2¼ cups powdered sugar, sifted

Drained canned crushed pineapple (from one 8-ounce can)

1½ cups finely chopped roasted cashews

6 pieces crystallized ginger, halved

(recipe continues)

1. Preheat the oven to 350°F. Lightly coat two 9-inch round cake pans with cooking spray. Set one of the pans on top of a doubled piece of parchment paper and trace around the bottom. Cut along the tracing to make 2 rounds of parchment. Place a parchment round in each pan, then lightly coat the top. Set the pans aside.

2. Whisk the flour, baking powder, baking soda, cinnamon, allspice, ginger, and salt together in a medium bowl.

3. Whisk the eggs and brown sugar together in a large bowl until the mixture is pale and creamy, about 30 seconds. Add the carrots, cashews, ginger, pineapple juice, vanilla, coconut oil, and CannaOil or CannaButter and whisk to combine. Add the flour mixture and stir until no dry streaks are visible.

4. Divide the batter between the two prepared cake pans and smooth the tops. Bake the cakes until the centers resist light pressure and a cake tester inserted into the center comes out clean, 25 to 28 minutes. Let the cakes cool in the pans on a wire rack for 30 minutes, then turn them out onto the wire rack to cool completely. Remove the parchment rounds.

5. **MAKE THE FROSTING:** Combine the butter and cream cheese in a stand mixer fitted with the paddle attachment and beat on medium speed until light and airy, about 2 minutes, using a rubber spatula to scrape the sides and bottom of the bowl as needed. Add the powdered sugar and beat on low speed until combined, about 30 seconds, then increase the speed to medium-high and beat until light and airy, 1 to 2 minutes. Measure out 1¼ cups of the frosting, transfer to a medium bowl, and stir in the crushed pineapple.

6. Place the bottom cake layer on a plate and spread all of the pineapple frosting across the surface, leaving a ½-inch border around the edges. Place the second cake layer on top and frost the top and sides with the remaining plain cream cheese frosting. Decorate the sides with the chopped cashews and place small pieces of ginger around the edges (to mark where you will slice the cake). Refrigerate for at least 30 minutes before slicing and serving. (The cake can be refrigerated for several days before serving; leave it out at room temperature for 20 minutes before slicing.)

MY AUNTIE USED to make this wonderfully sticky-sweet pudding for us kids and you bet I was the first one waiting by the oven with a spoon. I just loved it hot and fresh, sweet and good. The sweet coconut topping that is sometimes called conkalonk, or slush, because it's so syrupy and sticky, is what makes it so special. The pudding, which really has more of a cakelike texture, is loaded with sweet potatoes and raisins and absorbs some of the topping. The whole package is incredibly delicious. At Christmas time we'd steam the pudding outside over a coal stove—I remember using dumpling dough to cover the baking dish to seal in the steam. The fire made the flavor that much more special.

STICKY SWEET POTATO PUDDING WITH COCONUT "CONKALONK" TOPPING

SERVES 12 (MAKES ONE 9 X 13-INCH PAN; 5 MG THC PER SERVING)

2 tablespoons unsalted butter, at room temperature, or coconut oil

2 coconuts, cracked and meat separated from the shell (see page 75)

2 cups demerara sugar

2 tablespoons vanilla extract

2 teaspoons almond extract

1 teaspoon fine sea salt

1½ cups fine yellow cornmeal

½ cup all-purpose flour

1 tablespoon freshly grated nutmeg

2 teaspoons ground cinnamon

2 tablespoons CannaButter (page 26) or CannaOil (page 25; preferably made with coconut oil)

3 pounds (4 to 5 medium) Jamaican yellow yams (page 39) or Japanese sweet potatoes, peeled and grated on the medium holes of a box grater

2 cups raisins

¾ cup unsweetened shredded coconut

l. Preheat the oven to 350°F. Use the butter to grease a 9 x 12-inch baking dish that is 2 to 3 inches deep. Set aside.

(recipe continues)

2. Place the coconut meat in a blender with 1 cup of the sugar and 4 cups cool water and blend on high speed until the coconut is pretty well combined with no big chunks remaining (it won't be silky smooth—it will still have a somewhat rough texture) and the sugar is dissolved in the coconut milk. Strain the coconut milk through a fine-mesh sieve into a large bowl, pressing on the solids to extract as much liquid as possible. Return the coconut meat to the blender, add 4 more cups water and the remaining 1 cup sugar, and blend and strain again. Discard any coconut meat in the sieve. Stir in the vanilla, almond extract, and salt.

3. Whisk together the cornmeal, flour, nutmeg, and cinnamon in a large bowl. Measure out 6 cups of the coconut milk mixture (set the remaining coconut milk aside for later) and add to the bowl along with the CannaButter or CannaOil, grated yams, and raisins. Stir until combined.

4. Pour the batter into the prepared baking dish and bake until the edges are set, about 1 hour. Pour the reserved coconut milk over the top of the cake and bake until there are bubbles popping all across the surface of the cake, about 1 hour longer. Sprinkle with the shredded coconut and continue to bake until the coconut is golden, about 10 minutes. Remove from the oven and serve warm or at room temperature.

NOTE You can divide the recipe in half and bake it in a 9-inch square baking dish to serve fewer people. This is also an excellent make-ahead-and-freeze dessert to pull out as an impromptu bring-along to a dinner party!

CHEESECAKE IS PURE NICENESS, RIGHT? I top mine with a passion fruit gel made with agar-agar instead of gelatin. Agar-agar is made from seaweed and is a cleaner choice for your body than gelatin. You can find it in the aisle at the grocery store or health food store where you find other Japanese items like nori and pickled plums (it usually comes in a small pouch and almost looks like crumbly chalk). Cheesecake is a great dessert for feeding large groups—it's relatively quick to make and can be made in advance (a few days ahead is fine—just keep it chillin' in the fridge), making your life as a host so much easier. Keep in mind that this isn't one of those light and airy cheesecakes—this cheesecake is rich and dense and indulgent! I like to serve it at brunch, lunch, or early dinner rather than after supper late at night.

MARLEY PASSION CHEESECAKE

SERVES 12 (5 MG THC PER SERVING)

GRAHAM CRUST

2 cups graham cracker crumbs (from about 14 full crackers)

¼ teaspoon fine sea salt

7 tablespoons unsalted butter, melted

CHEESECAKE FILLING

24 ounces cream cheese or Neufchâtel (reduced-fat cream cheese), at room temperature

¾ cup granulated cane sugar

¼ teaspoon fine sea salt

Grated zest of 1 lime

⅓ cup heavy cream

2 tablespoons CannaOil (page 25), made with coconut oil

1 vanilla bean, split lengthwise

3 large cage-free eggs

PASSION GLAZE

⅔ cup passion fruit juice

1½ teaspoons agar-agar powder

1 teaspoon fresh lime juice

Whipped cream, for serving (optional)

1. **MAKE THE GRAHAM CRUST:** Preheat the oven to 350°F.

2. Combine the graham cracker crumbs and salt in a medium bowl. Use a fork to stir the crumbs while you pour in the melted butter, stirring until all of the crumbs are moistened, then turn them out into a 9-inch springform pan. Use the bottom of a

measuring cup to spread the crumbs into an even layer across the bottom of the pan and up the sides too, then use the measuring cup to pat them down so they are compact.

3. Place the crust in the oven and bake for 10 minutes. Remove from the oven and set aside. Leave the oven on, but reduce the oven temperature to 325°F. Once the pan is cool enough to handle, wrap the bottom with foil.

4. **MAKE THE CHEESECAKE FILLING:** In a stand mixer fitted with the paddle attachment, beat the cream cheese, sugar, salt, and lime zest together on medium speed, stopping the mixer to scrape down the sides and bottom of the bowl as needed, until the sugar is no longer grainy, 1 to 2 minutes. Add the cream and CannaOil and then use the tip of a knife to scrape the vanilla seeds into the bowl. Beat until well combined. Add the eggs, one at a time, mixing well after each addition.

5. Pour the filling into the crust and bake the cheesecake until the edges are set but the center jiggles slightly when the pan is tapped, about 1 hour. Turn off the oven and open the oven door a crack. Leave the cheesecake in the oven for 30 minutes. Remove the cake from the oven and cool to room temperature, 3 to 4 hours. Refrigerate until chilled.

6. **MAKE THE PASSION GLAZE:** Bring the passion fruit juice and agar-agar powder to a boil in a small saucepan set over high heat. Once it comes to a boil, reduce to a simmer and cook on medium-high for 30 seconds (otherwise the agar-agar will not set the topping), then remove from the heat and stir in the lime juice. Pour the mixture into a medium bowl and cool 5 minutes, then pour the topping over the cooled cheesecake, tilting the cake to spread it evenly.

7. Refrigerate the cheesecake for at least 8 hours or overnight. To serve, run a paring knife around the edges of the pan and release the springform sides. Cut the cheesecake into wedges and serve with dollops of whipped cream, if using.

I'VE ALWAYS HAD A THING FOR DONUTS. When I went to an all-girls Catholic school in Kingston sometimes we'd get a jelly donut for a snack after school as a special treat. Now I make a pumpkin-ginger version extra special by adding a bit of CannaOil to the batter! These are much healthier than the fried donuts we ate as kids since they're baked. Coffee and molasses give them a ton of flavor and moistness, making these special enough for a weekend breakfast treat or an afternoon coffee break. If you have a donut pan, here's a great excuse to *bruk out*! But hey now, don't think these are just for breakfast—arrange them on a cake stand and serve as a fun dessert—I can't think of anyone who would turn down a donut after dinner!

BAKED AND GLAZED PUMPKIN-GINGER DONUTS

IIIIIIIIIII MAKES 12 SMALL DONUTS (2 DONUTS PER SERVING; 5 MG THC PER SERVING) IIIIIIIIIII

DONUTS

4½ cups all-purpose flour

2 teaspoons baking powder

½ teaspoon baking soda

1½ teaspoons ground ginger

1 teaspoon ground cinnamon

½ teaspoon ground allspice

¾ teaspoon fine sea salt

½ cup canned pumpkin purée (not pumpkin pie filling)

4 tablespoons unsalted butter, melted

2 tablespoons CannaButter (page 26) or CannaOil (page 25)

1 cup lightly packed light brown sugar

2 large cage-free eggs

3 tablespoons very strong brewed coffee (espresso is perfect), at room temperature

¼ cup sour cream

3 tablespoons molasses

1 teaspoon vanilla extract

GLAZE

1 cup powdered sugar, sifted

½ teaspoon ground cinnamon

2 tablespoons canned pumpkin purée

1 teaspoon vanilla extract

Crushed gingersnap cookies (optional)

1. **MAKE THE DONUTS:** Preheat the oven to 425°F. Line a rimmed baking sheet with parchment paper.

(recipe continues)

2. Whisk together 3 cups of the flour, the baking powder, baking soda, ginger, cinnamon, allspice, and salt in a medium bowl.

3. Whisk together the pumpkin purée, 2 tablespoons of the melted butter, and the CannaButter or CannaOil in a large bowl. Whisk in the brown sugar followed by the eggs, one at a time. Whisk in the coffee, sour cream, molasses, and vanilla. Add the flour mixture to the pumpkin mixture and use a wooden spoon to stir until it is mostly combined (a few dry spots are okay). The dough will be very soft and sticky but don't worry—that's where the remaining 1½ cups flour comes in! (If using a donut pan, see the note at the end of the recipe and skip forward to step 7.)

4. Spread 1 cup of flour onto a work surface and place the dough on top. Sprinkle the remaining ½ cup of flour over the top of the dough. Use your hands and very light pressure to press the dough into a ½- to ¾-inch-thick sheet, coating your hands and the sides of the dough with flour from the work surface as needed to prevent sticking.

5. Use a 2¼-inch round biscuit cutter (or an overturned glass dipped in flour) to stamp out as many rounds as possible. Use a ¾-inch round cutter (or bottle cap) to stamp out the center from each round. Set the donuts on the prepared baking sheet. Gently press the scraps and donut holes together, taking care not to knead them too much (or the dough will toughen). Repeat, stamping out as many donuts as possible.

6. Brush the tops of the donuts with the remaining 2 tablespoons melted butter. Bake the donuts until they bounce back to light pressure, about 10 minutes. Remove from the oven and set aside while you make the glaze (it's best to glaze the donuts while they are still warm).

7. **MAKE THE GLAZE:** Whisk together the powdered sugar and cinnamon in a small bowl. Whisk in the pumpkin purée and vanilla until smooth. Dip the top of each warm donut into the glaze, sprinkle with crushed gingersnaps (if using), and serve warm.

NOTE If using a donut pan, after mixing the dough in step 3, divide the dough into 12 equal pieces, then press each into the donut pan. Bake the donuts until they are golden-brown and a cake tester inserted into one comes out clean, 8 to 10 minutes. Remove the donuts from the oven and let them cool in the pan for 5 minutes before turning them out onto a wire rack. Glaze while still warm.

POT BROWNIES: THE ORIGINAL EDIBLES! You've probably had pot brownies, but none like these decadent truffles. I make them by cutting brownies into squares, rolling them into two-bite balls, and then dipping into melted chocolate and coconut oil. As the chocolate cools, the shell hardens so when you bite into it the coating snaps. Talk about food that's fun to eat! Sometimes I sprinkle a little flaky sea salt, like fleur de sel (or smoked fleur de sel) on the coating before it hardens for that sweet-salty taste. These are awesome for getting a party started—why not give your guests a little sweet something with their cocktail? Rules were meant to be broken, am I right?

DOUBLE-CHOCOLATE BROWNIE TRUFFLES

IIIIIIIIIIIIIIII MAKES 24 TRUFFLES (2 TRUFFLES PER SERVING; 5 MG THC PER SERVING) IIIIIIIIIIIIIIII

BROWNIES

4 tablespoons unsalted butter

4 tablespoons CannaButter (page 26)

8 ounces bittersweet chocolate (at least 65% cacao), finely chopped

1 cup all-purpose flour

2 tablespoons Dutch process cocoa powder

½ teaspoon fine sea salt

3 large cage-free eggs

½ cup dark brown sugar

⅓ cup granulated cane sugar

2 tablespoons molasses

2 teaspoons vanilla extract

CHOCOLATE COATING

9 ounces bittersweet or semisweet chocolate, finely chopped

3 tablespoons coconut oil

1. Preheat the oven to 350°F. Lightly coat an 8-inch square baking pan with cooking spray. Fold a long piece of parchment paper or foil lengthwise to fit the pan, allowing the ends to extend over the sides of the pan. Lightly grease the parchment or foil.

2. MAKE THE BROWNIES: Place the butter, CannaButter, and chocolate in a heatproof bowl. Fill a medium saucepan with 2 inches of water and bring it to a simmer over high heat. Reduce the heat to low and set the bowl with the butter and chocolate over the simmering water (make sure the bottom of the bowl doesn't touch the water) and stir

(recipe continues)

often until the butter and chocolate are melted and smooth. Remove the bowl from the saucepan and set aside.

3. Whisk the flour, cocoa, and salt together in a medium bowl and set aside. Combine the eggs, brown sugar, granulated sugar, molasses, and vanilla in a large bowl and whisk until the mixture is thick and pale, about 1 minute of intense whisking. Whisk the chocolate mixture into the egg mixture and once combined, whisk in the flour mixture until no dry streaks remain.

4. Scrape the brownie batter into the prepared pan. Bake until a cake tester inserted into the center comes out with a few crumbs attached but no sticky batter, 20 to 22 minutes. Set the pan on a wire rack to cool completely.

5. Once the brownies are cool, use the ends of the parchment or foil to lift the brownies out of the pan. Trim the edges off the brownies (save these to make brownie crumbs to sprinkle over ice cream or for snacks). Slice the brownies lengthwise into 6 equal strips and then each crosswise into 4 pieces (24 small pieces total). Roll each piece into a ball (dampen your hands to prevent sticking).

6. **MAKE THE CHOCOLATE COATING:** Combine the chopped chocolate and coconut oil in a heatproof bowl. Fill a medium saucepan with 2 inches of water and bring it to a simmer over high heat. Reduce the heat to low and set the bowl with the coconut oil and chocolate over the simmering water (make sure the bottom of the bowl doesn't touch the water) and stir often until the chocolate is melted and the oil and chocolate are smoothly combined. Remove the bowl from the saucepan.

7. Working quickly (before the chocolate-oil mixture has time to cool), balance a brownie ball on a fork and dunk it into the magic shell to coat it completely. Lift it out, letting the excess coating drip off back into the bowl, then place it on a piece of parchment or wax paper. Repeat with the remaining brownie balls. (If the coating cools too much and gets hard, rewarm. Return the water to a simmer, set the bowl over the water, and stir occasionally until the mixture is fluid once again.)

8. Chill the truffles in the refrigerator until the shell hardens, at least 15 minutes or up to 3 days. You can eat them chilled or let them sit out at room temperature for a bit before serving (if your room is very warm, the shell may soften and become sticky as the brownie comes to room temperature, so don't let them sit out too long).

OVALTINE BISCUITS are like Jamaica's Chips Ahoy. They were one of my favorite store-bought sweets as a kid, so coming up with a homemade version was fun. Brittle and not too sweet or too buttery, they get a hit of malt from the Ovaltine mix. Like cake, enhancing cookies is so very easy—just substitute some CannaButter or CannaOil (or CannaVanilla) for some of the butter or oil (or vanilla) in the recipe. If you want two cookies to constitute one serving (I mean, come on, just one cookie is a little sad, no?), that means that every cookie should have 2.5 mg of THC—which, if you're using CannaButter or CannaOil, comes to ¼ teaspoon per cookie . . . so for a batch of two dozen, well, you can figure out the math! And oh hey, keep those fingers out of the cookie dough . . . and no licking the spoon (unless you want to feel fine). Oh one more thing—even though you're baking the cookies at 350°F, the inside temperature of the cookie doesn't get that hot, so you don't need to worry about the THC burning off.

|||||||||||||||||||||||||||||||||||||||||||||||||||||||||||||||||||||||||||||||||||||||||||||||||||||||||||||||||||||||||||

OVALTINE BISCUITS

|||||||||||||||||| MAKES 24 COOKIES (2 COOKIES PER SERVING; 5 MG THC PER SERVING) ||||||||||||||||||

1 stick plus 6 tablespoons (7 ounces) unsalted butter, at room temperature

2 tablespoons CannaButter (page 26) or CannaOil (page 25), at room temperature

¾ cup granulated cane sugar

2 cups all-purpose flour

½ cup Ovaltine

1 teaspoon fine sea salt

3 tablespoons heavy cream

2 large cage-free egg yolks

1 teaspoon vanilla extract

1 cup coarse demerara sugar

1. Combine the butter, CannaButter or CannaOil, and sugar in a stand mixer fitted with a paddle attachment and beat until the butter is light and airy, scraping down the sides and bottom of the bowl as needed, about 2 minutes.

2. Whisk the flour, Ovaltine, and salt together in a medium bowl. Whisk the cream, egg yolks, and vanilla together in a small bowl.

3. With the mixer running, add the flour mixture in 3 additions alternating with the cream mixture. Turn off the mixture and scrape down the sides and bottom of the bowl.

4. Place half of the dough on a long sheet of plastic wrap and roll it into a cylinder about 5 inches long and 2 inches wide and wrap tightly in plastic. Roll the cylinder back and forth to smooth out the sides so that when sliced, you'll have nice rounds. Repeat with the remaining dough. Refrigerate the logs for at least 2 hours or up to 3 days (or freeze up to 3 months).

5. Preheat the oven to 375°F. Line a baking sheet with parchment paper.

6. Remove the cookie logs from the refrigerator and unwrap them. Let them warm up at room temperature for 5 to 10 minutes (depending on how warm your room is). Place the demerara sugar on a plate and roll the log in the sugar to coat the entire surface. Set the log on a cutting board and slice into 12 cookies. Place the cookies on the prepared baking sheet and bake until they are golden and firm to light pressure, for 15 to 18 minutes, rotating the pan midway through baking. Cool the cookies for a few minutes on the pan, then transfer them to a wire rack to cool completely. Repeat with the second log and remaining demerara sugar.

MILO CHILL

Though biscuits flavored with Ovaltine—the malt powder that gets stirred into milk or water—were one of my favorite cookies as a child, we never drank Ovaltine at home. Instead we had Milo, another chocolate malt beverage. In the morning while the grownups were drinking their warm mint tea (page 83), we kids would be having our warm Milo. Sometimes when I'm nostalgic I'll make myself a warm mug of Milo and watch an old black-and-white movie. Add some CannaOil and feel pure niceness . . . so sweet.

7

NATURAL
BEAUTY

People are often asking me the secret to my "glowy" complexion and healthy skin. Well, the truth is this: I exercise a lot, which helps to flush out toxins and I make my own face and body scrubs, masks, and hair conditioning treatments, all from real ingredients that I have in my pantry (sometimes including CannaOil). Many of these homemade formulas have inspired the products in our Marley Natural skincare line. If you are a do-it-yourselfer, these are easy and fun to make yourself, and so much better for your wellness than many of the products you'll find in stores. You wouldn't eat food loaded with chemicals and fake fragrances . . . so why do you want to put a face mask or scrub with chemicals on your skin? Remember, skin absorbs everything you put on it, including all of those undesirable ingredients on the product label like parabens and preservatives. I don't rely on chemicals to have great skin and hair and neither should you.

READY TO RELAX?

Incorporating Herb into your life can be about treating yourself, about doing something kind, good, and *natural* for your body and soul. After making one of the treatments below, set the scene by putting on some chill music, dimming the lights, sparking some candles, and setting your phone to silent. Tuning out for a bit gives your body and mind a chance to recharge and reflect. Using an Herb-enhanced rub, lotion, or scrub won't bring on the psychotropic effects that ingesting Herb does, but it is known to be a great way to relax muscle tensions and reduce inflammation. There are also studies that claim that THC-infused topicals are very helpful for those who have autoimmune issues and psoriasis . . . there's no harm in trying one out to see if it helps!

Here is a list of ingredients you probably already have in your home and how they benefit your hair and skin.

INGREDIENT	BENEFIT
Aloe Vera (preferably fresh)	Moisturizer
Banana	Potassium makes for a great moisturizer, vitamin C for glow, fights fine lines
Castor Oil	Ricinoleic acid and omega-6 to accelerate hair growth; fights dandruff
Coarse Brown Sugar (like demerara)	Good body exfoliator for dry skin
Coconut Oil	Moisturizer, antibacterial, and makeup remover
Cucumber	Natural toner and astringent, hydrates skin, brightens complexion, soothes puffy eyes
Hemp Seed Oil	One of the best moisturizers around, loaded with linoleic acid; doesn't clog pores; great for redness and irritation
Hemp Seeds	Excellent facial exfoliator (without being overly abrasive), soothes irritated skin
Honey	Moisturizer and antibacterial
Lemon Juice	Antioxidants, vitamin C, and citric acid to fight aging; also brightens skin
Mayonnaise	Shiny hair

SKIN GLOW SCRUB

||||||||||||||||||||||||||||||||||||||||||||||||||||||| MAKES 1 APPLICATION |||||||||||||||||||||||||||||||||||||||||||||||||||||||

1 tablespoon organic honey

1 tablespoon coconut oil or hemp seed oil

½ teaspoon CannaOil (optional; page 25)

1 tablespoon hulled hemp seeds

Squeeze of fresh lemon juice

Mix all of the ingredients together until they form a paste. Apply to your face in circular motions and leave on for 15 to 20 minutes. Rinse off with warm water, then gently pat your skin dry. (If you have a darker complexion, try adding 1 teaspoon ground turmeric to the scrub for extra glow; note that for pale complexions, the turmeric can stain your skin yellow!)

STRONG SHINE HAIR TREATMENT

||||||||||||||||||||||||||||||||||||||||||||||||||||||| MAKES 1 APPLICATION |||||||||||||||||||||||||||||||||||||||||||||||||||||||

¼ cup mayonnaise

¼ cup castor oil

Whisk the mayonnaise and oil together in a small bowl. Apply to dry hair, working it into the roots and your scalp first, then drawing out to the ends of your hair. Cover your hair with a shower cap, a cloth scarf, or a plastic bag (sometimes I like to use a warm towel too for extra penetration into the hair shaft) and treat your hair for at least 30 minutes or overnight. When you get into the shower, don't wash your hair right away—first work a good palmful of shampoo into your hair, massaging it into your scalp for a few minutes before rinsing and conditioning as usual.

NOTE My family has created a line of body-care products combining naturally derived formulas of cold-pressed hemp seed oil (without any psychoactive THC or CBD) and Jamaican botanicals like rosemary, lemongrass, and cerasse (a medicinal and very bitter herb also known as "bush tea"). All of our Marley Natural skincare products are paraben-, sulfate-, and cruelty-free and all reflect the Marley ethos of positivity, progress, and natural well-being.

PUMPKIN FACE SCRUB

2 tablespoons canned organic pumpkin purée (not pumpkin pie filling!)

1 teaspoon coconut oil or hemp seed oil

½ teaspoon CannaOil (optional; page 25)

1 tablespoon oat flour (or finely ground rolled oats)

1 teaspoon organic dark or light brown sugar (use the organic sugar—it has a coarser texture)

¼ teaspoon ground cinnamon

¼ teaspoon freshly grated nutmeg

¼ teaspoon ground allspice

Mix all of the ingredients together. Apply to your face and leave on for 5 to 10 minutes, then rub the scrub into your face in a circular motion for 30 seconds to 1 minute. Rinse off with warm water, then gently pat your skin dry.

BANANA-HONEY FACE MASK

1 ripe banana, peeled

1 tablespoon honey

½ teaspoon CannaOil (optional; page 25)

½ teaspoon fresh lemon juice

Place the banana, honey, CannaOil (if using), and lemon juice in a small bowl and use a fork to mash and stir it until smooth. Apply the mask to your face and let it sit for 15 minutes. Use a warm washcloth to remove the mask and rinse your face with warm water, then gently pat your skin dry.

ALOE AND SUGAR BODY SCRUB

¼ cup coarse brown sugar (such as demerara)

1 tablespoon extra-virgin olive oil or hemp seed oil

½ teaspoon CannaOil (optional; page 25)

1 tablespoon aloe vera gel (or fresh aloe, see below)

Combine the brown sugar, olive oil, CannaOil (if using), and aloe vera gel in a small bowl and mix together well. Apply to your body and face using a circular motion to exfoliate. Rinse off, alternating between cold and warm water, then gently pat your skin dry.

EXTRACTING FRESH ALOE

Carefully remove a long aloe leaf from the plant by cutting it at an angle at the base of the stalk (the middle leaves are thicker and contain the most gel). Let the leaf rest in an upright position, cut side down, for 15 minutes, then wash the leaf to remove any leftover sap. Place the leaf on a cutting board, remove any thorny edges, then halve the leaf lengthwise and use a spoon to scoop out the gel from inside the leaf. Whatever gel you don't use can be refrigerated in an airtight glass jar for up to 1 year.

CITRUS-GINGER SUGAR SCRUB

2 tablespoons grated fresh ginger

1 tablespoon fresh lime juice

½ cup organic dark or light brown sugar
(use the organic sugar—it has a coarser
texture)

¼ cup coconut oil or hemp seed oil

1 teaspoon CannaOil (optional; page 25)

Combine the ginger, lime juice, brown sugar, coconut oil, and CannaOil (if using) in a medium bowl. Using an electric hand mixer or a whisk, beat the mixture until it is very airy and fluffy, about 2 minutes. Transfer the mixture to a glass jar. Use in the shower, scrubbing into your skin, and refrigerate whatever is left over to use another time (the scrub is best used within 5 days).

ALOE-HEMP EXFOLIATOR

½ small cucumber, peeled and grated on
the medium holes of a box grater
(¼ to ⅓ cup)

¼ to ⅓ cup aloe vera gel (about the same
amount as the cucumber)

3 tablespoons hulled hemp seeds

1 teaspoon CannaOil (optional; page 25)

Combine the grated cucumber and aloe in a small bowl until it forms a paste. Stir in the hemp seeds and CannaOil (if using) and spread the paste onto your face, using your hands to massage it into your skin in a circular motion. Let it sit on your face for 10 minutes. Rinse off under warm water and gently pat your skin dry.

OTHER WAYS TO CHILL WITH HERB

My mom has been using Herb in beauty treatments for decades. Here are a few of her tips for incorporating Herb into your overall health, beauty, and wellness routine.

SOAK IN IT: Steep some Herb in boiling hot water, then add it to your bath with some lavender, rose petals, eucalyptus, fever grass (lemongrass), and/or citrus rounds.

SCRUB WITH IT: Add some decarbed Herb (page 22) to the Aloe and Sugar Body Scrub (page 220).

DRINK IT: Add Herb to herbal tea (see page 83 for more on this).

STEAM IN IT: Add Herb to just-boiled hot water, set your face over the bowl, drape a towel over your head, and breathe in the steam.

SOOTHE AND SMOKE
WITH MARLEY NATURAL

HEMP-BASED BODY CARE: My family has created a line of body care products combining naturally derived formulas of cold-pressed hemp seed oil (without any psychoactive THC or CBD) and Jamaican botanicals like rosemary, lemongrass, and cerasse (a medicinal and very bitter herb also known as "bush tea"). All of our Marley Natural skincare products are paraben-, sulfate-, and cruelty-free and all reflect the Marley ethos of positivity, progress, and natural well-being.

GEAR AND ACCESSORIES: We all like to go old school once in a while. For anyone who still likes to toke up the old-fashioned way, Marley Natural offers sophisticated smoking products for discerning herb connoisseurs. The collection is made from sustainably grown American black walnut pieces accented by heat-resistant hand-blown glass. Check out the collection at marleynaturalshop.com.

MARLEY FAMILY FOOD PRODUCTS

Eating is important to my family and always has been. The quality of what we put into our bodies is vital, so a few of my siblings and I decided to launch our own product lines where we can control the purity and quality of a few key ingredients we use often in our kitchens.

MARLEY COFFEE: My brother Rohan packages sustainably grown and ethically farmed coffee with each roast named after one of Daddy's songs. The coffee is sourced from Ethiopia, Jamaica, and Central and South America and is roasted by hand—he even grows organic Blue Mountain coffee on the family's 52-acre farm in the parish of Portland. Rohan has partnered with Water Wise Coffee to help compost coffee pulp and reduce waste impact while helping support the people and communities where Marley Coffee is sourced.
marleycoffee.com

MARLEY KITCHEN: My family's line of sauces are also named after a few of Daddy's songs, like "Jammin'" jerk barbecue sauce, "Catch a Fire" Scotch bonnet pepper sauce, and "One Love" spicy tomato sauce. All are based on traditional Jamaican recipes. We're working with small family farms to ensure the pureness and quality of the sauces and also to carry on the sustainable movement as a family.

One percent of the sales from sauces contributes to creating a sustainable-income source for women and their children through farming initiatives under the Women Helping Others Achieve (WHOA) program. This program provides funding to build the capacity for women farmers through skills training, provision of seeds, shade and greenhouses, and necessary tools and equipment in Jamaica, Grenada, and Haiti.
themarleykitchen.com

COCO'MON: My brother Ziggy's cold-pressed, unrefined, and organic coconut oil. Comes in original coconut, lemon-ginger, and curry flavors.
ziggymarley.com

HEMP RULES: Ziggy's roasted and shelled organic hemp seeds. Comes in unseasoned original, sea salt and pepper, or Caribbean crunch flavors.
ziggymarley.com

ACKNOWLEDGMENTS

It is your family, your memories, and the life around you that nurtures the flow in your kitchen, that keeps the beat of your wooden spoon to the pan. I am so blessed to have had the opportunity to write this book and travel back in time to recall so many key moments. The sounds and tastes of my childhood in Jamaica represent my past, while my family gives me my rhythm in the kitchen today, defining my present. This book is a meeting of the two, and each recipe, like a song, captures time. By weaving Herb throughout the book we have breached a barrier, and have come to a threshold of enlightenment as we thoughtfully are more at one with ourselves and our Mother Earth.

THE WRITING: Thanks to Raquel Pelzel for the time you spent in my kitchen, for adapting to and adopting the Marley Natural culture and for deliciously bringing the words and recipes to paper.

THE PUBLISHER, PAM KRAUSS: Do all publishers put so much love, understanding, time, and patience into their projects? Truly apprecilove you for making it happen.

THE AGENTS: I have the best book agents! Susan Ginsburg and Barbara Marcus, thank you for finding such a wonderful home for my stories. We have more to go and I can't go it without you!

THE SHOOT: Aubrie Pick, aside from taking magnificent photos, you truly know how to make a location feel like home; and Bessma Khalaf for assisting. To producer Cortney Menna and assistant Sandra Garcia for managing it all, to Kate Martindale (and Ali, Brian, and Ross) for propping so stylishly, Brett Long for artfully presenting, and Hans Pena for assisting. Much love and respect to my very lovely and photogenic real-life family and friends for being my "brunch" and "dinner" guests. My brother Rohan and sister Karen, who keep me smiling and laughing throughout. Joseph—you are a star! And Leslie, brand manager by day and beautiful party guest by night. Lois for getting me there, for being there and keeping it moving. To Aunt Del, whose red lipstick was the highlight of my days. And to you, Jahkyra, so glad to have you there for every slice, pinch, and stitch—for every dish and every thought of the day . . . love you!

THE LOOK: stylists Hachy Mendez, Anastasia Clemens, and Raquel; lead makeup artist Melissa Hibbert and Patrick Johnson; and hairstylist Kimm Epps, thank you for putting it all together and keeping me laughing.

THE CREW: To those who support me in all that I do—Paul, Doreen, Courtney, Tyler, Mike, Chuck, Irina, Marie, Myshjua, Karl, and all the team members at the Bob Marley Museum, Tuff Gong International, Bob Marley Foundation, Rita Marley Foundation, and Tuff Gong Worldwide.

THE PARTNERS: To the Marley Natural team who really overstand that "Herb is a plant" with the ability to heal, nurture, and transform. Your dedication and passion to making positive changes truly inspires me daily. Also to Philippe Lucas and Chris McDonough, and Keith Moen at Tilray and Privateer: Your expertise is unequaled (and thank you to Martha Holmberg for allowing your kitchen to turn into our Portland test kitchen for a spell).

THE PEOPLE WHO GET MARLEY KITCHEN, MARLEY COFFEE, AND HOUSE OF MARLEY ONTO SHELVES: Thank you for working tirelessly, supporting Jamaica, our farming community, our traditions, and your commitment to sustainability.

THE FAMILY: Sharon, Ziggy, Stephen, Rohan, Robbie, Ky-mani, Karen, Stephanie, Julian, and Damian; you were my best friends growing up and are my best friends as a grownup. Thank you for your love, support, and for being there for me always. To my brilliant and talented nieces and nephews, you are our future and I love you all. Uncle Taddy, who introduced me to the great annatto seed; Orly for always making sure I was taken care of when in her yard; Aunt Viola for showing me how to steam Christmas puddings over a coal fire; and Grandma Booker, who taught me how to make tofu taste like chicken!

TO DANNY, SOUL-REBEL, SKIP, AND SAIYAN. My four heartbearts.

AND TO MY PARENTS: Thank you for creating me.

INDEX

Page numbers in *italics* refer to photos.

A

"About'a Turn" Mango Salad, *120,* 129

All-In Macaroni and Cheese, 156–57

Aloe and Sugar Body Scrub, 220

Aloe-Hemp Exfoliator, *222, 223*

apples

Hemp, Kale, and Apple Salad, 126, *127*

Marley Family Green Juice, 91

avocados

Guacamole with Fried Plantain Chips, 110–13, *111*

Hemp Guacamole (variation), 101

Island Beet Burgers with Avocado and Jerk-Fried Onions, 167–69, *168*

Superpowered Hemp Dip, 101

B

Babaghanouj Mashup, 109

Bagels, Smoke Ring Stuffed, *76,* 77

Baked and Glazed Pumpkin-Ginger Donuts, *204,* 205–6

bananas

Banana Fritters, 68–69, *69*

Banana-Honey Face Mask, 219

Cedella's Spirulina Smoothie, *92,* 93

Curry Rundown with Boiled Green Banana, *72,* 73–74

Guava Cream Cheese–Stuffed Banana Muffins, 63–64, *65*

Barbecue Sauce, Tamarind, Grilled Jerk Chicken with, *140,* 141–42

beans

Gungo Rice 'n Peas, 185–86, *187*

Island Beet Burgers with Avocado and Jerk-Fried Onions, 167–69, *168*

Ital Stew with Spinners, 173–74, *175*

Jerk Tofu Taco with Black Bean–Mango Salsa, 164–66, *165*

Rice 'n Red Peas (variation), 186

beauty treatments

Aloe and Sugar Body Scrub, 220

Aloe-Hemp Exfoliator, *222, 223*

Banana-Honey Face Mask, 219

Citrus-Ginger Sugar Scrub, *222, 223*

to incorporate herb into, 224

ingredients, 215

Pumpkin Face Scrub, 218, *218*

Skin Glow Scrub, 216, *217*

Strong Shine Hair Treatment, 216

beets

Fresh Beet "Hummus" with Homemade Pita Chips, 107–9, *108*

greens, to cook, 135

Island Beet Burgers with Avocado and Jerk-Fried Onions, 167–69, *168*

Spinach Salad with Goat Cheese, Pickled Beets, and Pine Nuts, 133–35, *134*

bell peppers

Curry with Ritty Roti, *160,* 161–63

Grilled Jerk Vegetables with Lime Vinaigrette, 123–25

Homemade Caribbean-Style Vegetable Broth, 180

Island Beet Burgers with Avocado and Jerk-Fried Onions, 167–69, *168*

Jerk Tofu Taco with Black Bean–Mango Salsa, 164–66, *165*

Pepperpot Soup, 178–80, *179*

Pickle Me This, Pickle Me That, 116, *117*

Saltfish Fritters with Fiery Dippin' Sauce, 118–19

Snapper Escovitch, 139

beverages

Catch a Star Juice, *96,* 97

Cedella's Spirulina Smoothie, *92,* 93

Chilled Sorrel Punch, 88, *89*

cocoa tea, *84,* 85

herb in, 82, 86

Irish moss in, 94

Marley Family Green Juice, 91

Morning Mint Tea, *80,* 83

beverages *(continued)*
    Passion Juice, 95
    tonics, 90
    Warm Sorrel Punch, 89
blueberries, *in* Cedella's
    Spirulina Smoothie, *92, 93*
Boiled Green Banana, Curry
    Rundown with, *72, 73*–74
breakfast foods. *See* morning
    foods
broccoli, *in* Curry Rundown
    with Boiled Green Banana,
    72, 73–74
Broth, Homemade Caribbean-
    Style Vegetable, 180
Brownie Truffles, Double-
    Chocolate, 207–8, *209*
Burgers, Island Beet, with
    Avocado and Jerk-Fried
    Onions, 167–69, *168*

C
Cake, Gingery Carrot, with
    Pineapple and Cashews,
    196, 197–98
Callaloo and Smoky Gouda
    Fried Dumplings, 104–6,
    105
CannaButter, 26–28, *27,* 31
CannaOil, *24,* 25, 31
CannaVanilla Extract, 29
Caramel-Jerk Popcorn,
    Jammin', *98,* 102–3
Caribbean-Style Vegetable
    Broth, Homemade, 180
carrots
    Catch a Star Juice, *96,* 97
    Gingery Carrot Cake with
        Pineapple and Cashews,
        196, 197–98
    Ital Stew with Spinners,
        173–74, *175*
    Pepperpot Soup, 178–80, *179*
    Pickle Me This, Pickle Me
        That, 116, *117*

Cashews, Gingery Carrot Cake
    with Pineapple and, *196,*
    197–98
Cashews and Coconut, Curry,
    Quinoa with, 130–32, *131*
Catch a Star Juice, *96, 97*
cauliflower, *in* Pickle Me This,
    Pickle Me That, 116, *117*
Cedella's Spirulina Smoothie,
    92, 93
cheddar cheese
    All-In Macaroni and
        Cheese, 156–57
    Triple-Threat Spicy Corn
        Bake, *182,* 183–84
Cheesecake, Marley Passion,
    202–3
Chicken, Grilled Jerk, with
    Tamarind Barbecue Sauce,
    140, 141–42
Chicken, Oven-Barbecued
    (variation), 142
Chips, Fried Plantain,
    Guacamole with, 110–13,
    111
Chips, Homemade Pita, Fresh
    Beet "Hummus" with,
    107–9, *108*
Chocolate Brownie Truffles,
    Double-, 207–8, *209*
Citrus-Ginger Sorbet with
    Raise-Up Raspberry Sauce,
    194–95
Citrus-Ginger Sugar Scrub,
    222, 223
cocoa tea, *84, 85*
coconut, fresh, to use, 75
Coconut, Quinoa with Curry
    Cashews and, 130–32, *131*
Coconut "Conkalonk"
    Topping, Sticky Sweet
    Potato Pudding with,
    199–200, *201*
Corn Bake, Triple-Threat
    Spicy, *182,* 183–84

Cornmeal Porridge, Jamaican,
    66, 67
cream cheese
    Gingery Carrot Cake with
        Pineapple and Cashews,
        196, 197–98
    Guava Cream Cheese–
        Stuffed Banana Muffins,
        63–64, *65*
    Marley Passion Cheesecake,
        202–3
    Smoke Ring Stuffed Bagels,
        76, 77
cucumbers
    Aloe-Hemp Exfoliator, *222,*
        223
    Marley Family Green Juice,
        91
    Pickle Me This, Pickle Me
        That, 116, *117*
    Smoke Ring Stuffed Bagels,
        76, 77
Curry Cashews and Coconut,
    Quinoa with,
    130–32, *131*
Curry Rundown with Boiled
    Green Banana, *72, 73*–74
Curry with Ritty Roti, *160,*
    161–63

D
desserts
    Baked and Glazed
        Pumpkin-Ginger
        Donuts, *204,* 205–6
    Citrus-Ginger Sorbet with
        Raise-Up Raspberry
        Sauce, 194–95
    Double-Chocolate Brownie
        Truffles, 207–8, *209*
    fast and easy enhanced ice
        cream, 192
    Gingery Carrot Cake with
        Pineapple and Cashews,
        196, 197–98

Marley Passion Cheesecake, 202–3
Ovaltine Biscuits, 210–11
Rum Raisin and Grape-Nuts Ice Cream, 191–92, *193*
Sticky Sweet Potato Pudding with Coconut "Conkalonk" Topping, 199–200, *201*
Dip, Superpowered Hemp, 101
Dippin' Sauce, Fiery, Saltfish Fritters with, 118–19
Donuts, Baked and Glazed Pumpkin-Ginger, *204,* 205–6
Double-Chocolate Brownie Truffles, 207–8, *209*
drinks. *See* beverages
Dumplings, Callaloo and Smoky Gouda Fried, 104–6, *105*
Dumplings, Hemp Seed Fried, 78

E

eggplant, *in* Grilled Jerk Vegetables with Lime Vinaigrette, 123–25
entertaining. *See* party foods
Escovitch, Snapper, 139
Exfoliator, Aloe-Hemp, *222,* 223

F

face care products. *See* beauty treatments
Festival, Red Stripe Battered Fish 'n, 143–44, *145*
Fiery Dippin' Sauce, Saltfish Fritters with, 118–19
fish
   Red Stripe Battered Fish 'n Festival, 143–44, *145*
   Saltfish Fritters with Fiery Dippin' Sauce, 118–19
Saltfish One-Pot, 176–77
Smoke Ring Stuffed Bagels, *76, 77*
Snapper Escovitch, 139
Fresh Beet "Hummus" with Homemade Pita Chips, 107–9, *108*
Fried Dumplings, Callaloo and Smoky Gouda, 104–6, *105*
Fried Dumplings, Hemp Seed, 78
Fried Plantain Chips, Guacamole with, 110–13, *111*
Fritters, Banana, 68–69, *69*
Fritters, Saltfish, with Fiery Dippin' Sauce, 118–19

G

Garlic Salt, 49
Gingery Carrot Cake with Pineapple and Cashews, *196,* 197–98
Goat Cheese, Pickled Beets, and Pine Nuts, Spinach Salad with, 133–35, *134*
Gouda cheese
   Callaloo and Smoky Gouda Fried Dumplings, 104–6, *105*
   My Veg Lasagna, 152–55, *154*
Grape-Nuts and Rum Raisin Ice Cream, 191–92, *193*
Green Banana, Boiled, Curry Rundown with, *72,* 73–74
Green Juice, Marley Family, 91
green peas
   Curry with Ritty Roti, *160,* 161–63
   Island Potato Salad, 181
grinders, 23
Grilled Jerk Chicken with Tamarind Barbecue Sauce, *140,* 141–42
Grilled Jerk Vegetables with Lime Vinaigrette, 123–25
Gruyère cheese, *in* All-In Macaroni and Cheese, 156–57
Guacamole, Hemp (variation), 101
Guacamole with Fried Plantain Chips, 110–13, *111*
Guava Cream Cheese-Stuffed Banana Muffins, 63–64, *65*
Guava Ketchup, Smoky Baked Yuca Wedges with, 114–15
Gungo Rice 'n Peas, 185–86, *187*

H

Hair Treatment, Strong Shine, 216
hemp seeds
   Aloe-Hemp Exfoliator, *222, 223*
   Hemp, Kale, and Apple Salad, 126, *127*
   Hemp Guacamole (variation), 101
   Hemp Pesto, 50, *51*
   Hemp Seed Fried Dumplings, 78
   Skin Glow Scrub, 216, *217*
   Superpowered Hemp Dip, 101
Herb
   to decarboxylate, 19, 22
   grinders, 23
   growing conditions, 79, 122, 170
   Jamaican Lambsbread strain, 29
   kief and trichomes, 21, 22, 64
   purchasing at dispensaries, 19

Herb (continued)
 in Rastafari way of life, 9
 sativa and indica strains, 19
 spiritual and medicinal
  benefits, 10–13, 15, 18,
  70, 158, 170
 sugar trim, 21, 30
 terpenes, 170
 THC dose per serving of
  edibles, 20–22, 30–31,
  53–54
 using responsibly, 58–59,
  113
Herb-Sesame Salt, 48
Homemade Caribbean-Style
 Vegetable Broth, 180
"Hummus," Fresh Beet, with
 Homemade Pita Chips,
 107–9, *108*

I

ice cream, fast and easy
 enhancements for, 192
Ice Cream, Rum Raisin and
 Grape-Nuts, 191–92, *193*
Irish moss, to use in drinks, 94
Island Beet Burgers with
 Avocado and Jerk-Fried
 Onions, 167–69, *168*
Island Potato Salad, 181
Ital Stew with Spinners,
 173–74, *175*

J

Jamaican Cornmeal Porridge,
 66, 67
Jamaican culture and foods
 bammy, 115
 cinnamon leaves, 66
 cocoa tea, *84,* 85
 gungo peas, 186
 Irish moss, 94
 mint tea, 83
 pantry staples, 37–41
 Rastafari way of life, 9, 17

 slang, 41
 traditional dishes, 37, 78,
  143, 147, 176
 vibrancy and positivity, 33
Jamaican Patties, Spicy, *146,*
 147–49
Jammin' Caramel-Jerk
 Popcorn, *98,* 102–3
Jerk Chicken, Grilled, with
 Tamarind Barbecue Sauce,
 140, 141–42
Jerk-Fried Onions, Island Beet
 Burgers with Avocado and,
 167–69, *168*
Jerk Paste, 46
Jerk Seasoning, 45
Jerk Tofu Taco with Black
 Bean–Mango Salsa, 164–66,
 165
Jerk Vegetables, Grilled, with
 Lime Vinaigrette, 123–25
Johnnycakes (Hemp Seed Fried
 Dumplings), 78
juices and smoothies. *See*
 beverages

K

kale
 Hemp, Kale, and Apple
  Salad, 126, *127*
 Marley Family Green Juice,
  91
Ketchup, Guava, Smoky Baked
 Yuca Wedges with, 114–15

L

Lasagna, My Veg, 152–55, *154*
Lasagna Wonton Cups,
 Individual (variation), 155
lox, *for* Smoke Ring Stuffed
 Bagels, *76, 77*

M

Macaroni and Cheese, All-In,
 156–57

mangoes
 "About'a Turn" Mango
  Salad, *120,* 129
 Jerk Tofu Taco with Black
  Bean–Mango Salsa,
  164–66, *165*
 Quinoa with Curry
  Cashews and Coconut,
  130–32, *131*
Marley, Bob, and family
 embrace of whole and
  natural foods, 34, 90, 91,
  95, 191
 happiness and positivity,
  10, 34, 158
 Rastafari philosophy and
  use of herb, 9–10, 15, 29,
  37, 82
Marley Family Green Juice, 91
Marley Natural brand and
 products, 17, 226, 229
Marley Passion Cheesecake,
 202–3
Mint Tea, Morning,
 80, 83
morning foods
 Banana Fritters, 68–69, *69*
 Curry Rundown with
  Boiled Green Banana, *72,*
  73–74
 Guava Cream Cheese–
  Stuffed Banana Muffins,
  63–64, *65*
 Hemp Seed Fried
  Dumplings, 78
 herb strains for, 62
 Jamaican Cornmeal
  Porridge, *66, 67*
 Morning Mint Tea,
  80, 83
 Saltfish Fritters, 118
 Smoke Ring Stuffed Bagels,
  76, 77
mozzarella cheese, *in* My Veg
 Lasagna, 152–55, *154*

Muffins, Banana, Guava Cream Cheese–Stuffed, 63–64, *65*
munchies
    Babaghanouj Mashup, 109
    Callaloo and Smoky Gouda Fried Dumplings, 104–6, *105*
    Fresh Beet "Hummus" with Homemade Pita Chips, 107–9, *108*
    Guacamole with Fried Plantain Chips, 110–13, *111*
    Hemp Guacamole (variation), 101
    Jammin' Caramel-Jerk Popcorn, *98,* 102–3
    Pickle Me This, Pickle Me That, 116, *117*
    Saltfish Fritters with Fiery Dippin' Sauce, 118–19
    Smoky Baked Yuca Wedges with Guava Ketchup, 114–15
    to spike, 100
    Superpowered Hemp Dip, 101
mushrooms
    Curry Rundown with Boiled Green Banana, *72,* 73–74
    Grilled Jerk Vegetables with Lime Vinaigrette, 123–25
    My Veg Lasagna, 152–55, *154*
My Veg Lasagna, 152–55, *154*

O

okra
    Curry Rundown with Boiled Green Banana, *72,* 73–74
    Pepperpot Soup, 178–80, *179*

One-Pot, Saltfish, 176–77
Onions, Jerk-Fried, Island Beet Burgers with Avocado and, 167–69, *168*
Ovaltine Biscuits, 210–11
Oven-Barbecued Chicken (variation), 142

P

Parmigiano-Reggiano cheese
    All-In Macaroni and Cheese, 156–57
    My Veg Lasagna, 152–55, *154*
party foods. *See also* munchies
    All-In Macaroni and Cheese, 156–57
    Curry with Ritty Roti, *160,* 161–63
    Grilled Jerk Chicken with Tamarind Barbecue Sauce, *140,* 141–42
    Gungo Rice 'n Peas, 185–86, *187*
    herb-enhanced parties, 16, 138, 151, 190
    Island Beet Burgers with Avocado and Jerk-Fried Onions, 167–69, *168*
    Island Potato Salad, 181
    Ital Stew with Spinners, 173–74, *175*
    Jerk Tofu Taco with Black Bean–Mango Salsa, 164–66, *165*
    menus, 56–57
    My Veg Lasagna, 152–55, *154*
    Pepperpot Soup, 178–80, *179*
    Red Stripe Battered Fish 'n Festival, 143–44, *145*
    Saltfish One-Pot, 176–77
    Snapper Escovitch, 139
    Spicy Jamaican Patties, *146,* 147–49

store-bought add-ons, 57
THC dosages, 20–22, 30–31, 53–54
Triple-Threat Spicy Corn Bake, *182,* 183–84
Passion Cheesecake, Marley, 202–3
Passion Juice, 95
pasta
    All-In Macaroni and Cheese, 156–57
    Individual Lasagna Wonton Cups (variation), 155
    My Veg Lasagna, 152–55, *154*
    Pesto Pasta Stuffed Vegetables (serving suggestion), 50
    Patties, Spicy Jamaican, *146,* 147–49
    Pepperpot Soup, 178–80, *179*
peppers, bell. *See* bell peppers
peppers, roasted, *in* My Veg Lasagna, 152–55, *154*
Pesto, Hemp, 50, *51*
Pesto Pasta Stuffed Vegetables (serving suggestion), 50
Pickle Me This, Pickle Me That, 116, *117*
pineapple
    Cedella's Spirulina Smoothie, *92, 93*
    Gingery Carrot Cake with Pineapple and Cashews, *196,* 197–98
    Marley Family Green Juice, 91
    Passion Juice, 95
Pine Nuts, Spinach Salad with Goat Cheese, Pickled Beets, and, 133–35, *134*

Pita Chips, Homemade, Fresh Beet "Hummus" with, 107–9, *108*

plantains
Guacamole with Fried Plantain Chips, 110–13, *111*
Ital Stew with Spinners, 173–74, *175*

Popcorn, Jammin' Caramel-Jerk, *98*, 102–3

Porridge, Jamaican Cornmeal, *66, 67*

potatoes
Curry with Ritty Roti, *160,* 161–63
Island Potato Salad, 181
Ital Stew with Spinners, 173–74, *175*

Pudding, Sticky Sweet Potato, with Coconut "Conkalonk" Topping, 199–200, *201*

Pumpkin Face Scrub, 218, *218*

Pumpkin-Ginger Donuts, Baked and Glazed, *204,* 205–6

Punch, Chilled Sorrel (and warm variation), 88–89, *89*

Q
Quinoa with Curry Cashews and Coconut, 130–32, *131*

R
Raise-Up Raspberry Sauce, Citrus-Ginger Sorbet with, 194–95

raisins
Rum Raisin and Grape-Nuts Ice Cream, 191–92, *193*
Sticky Sweet Potato Pudding with Coconut

"Conkalonk" Topping, 199–200, *201*

Raspberry Sauce, Raise-Up, Citrus-Ginger Sorbet with, 194–95

Red Peas, Rice 'n (variation), 186

Red Stripe Battered Fish 'n Festival, 143–44, *145*

rice
Gungo Rice 'n Peas, 185–86, *187*
Rice 'n Red Peas (variation), 186
Saltfish One-Pot, 176–77
Roti, Ritty, Curry with, *160,* 161–63

rum
Chilled Sorrel Punch, 88, *89*
Rum Raisin and Grape-Nuts Ice Cream, 191–92, *193*
Warm Sorrel Punch (variation), 89

S
salad dressings as gifts, 125

salads
"About'a Turn" Mango Salad, *120,* 129
Grilled Jerk Vegetables with Lime Vinaigrette, 123–25
Hemp, Kale, and Apple Salad, 126, *127*
Island Potato Salad, 181
Quinoa with Curry Cashews and Coconut, 130–32, *131*
Spinach Salad with Goat Cheese, Pickled Beets, and Pine Nuts, 133–35, *134*

Salsa, Black Bean–Mango, Jerk Tofu Taco with, 164–66, *165*

Saltfish Fritters with Fiery Dippin' Sauce, 118–19

Saltfish One-Pot, 176–77

sauces and salsa
Black Bean–Mango Salsa, 164–66, *165*
Fiery Dippin' Sauce, 118–19
as gifts, 125
Guava Ketchup, 114
Hemp Pesto, 50, *51*
Raise-Up Raspberry Sauce, 194
Tamarind Barbecue Sauce, 141

scrubs. *See* beauty treatments

seasonings and spiked seasonings
enhanced blends, 42
Garlic Salt, 49
Hemp Pesto, 50, *51*
Herb-Sesame Salt, 48
Jerk Paste, 46
Jerk Seasoning, 45
Smoke Salt, 47

seitan, *in* Island Beet Burgers with Avocado and Jerk-Fried Onions, 167–69, *168*

skincare products. *See* beauty treatments

Smoke Ring Stuffed Bagels, *76, 77*

Smoke Salt, 47

Smoky Baked Yuca Wedges with Guava Ketchup, 114–15

Smoky Gouda and Callaloo Fried Dumplings, 104–6, *105*

Smoothie, Cedella's Spirulina, *92, 93*

snacks. *See* munchies

Snapper Escovitch, 139

Sorbet, Citrus-Ginger, with Raise-Up Raspberry Sauce, 194–95

Sorrel Punch, Chilled (and warm variation), 88–89, *89*
Soup, Pepperpot, 178–80, *179*
Spicy Jamaican Patties, *146,* 147–49
spiked seasonings. *See* seasonings and spiked seasonings
spinach
    Callaloo and Smoky Gouda Fried Dumplings, 104–6, *105*
    Grilled Jerk Vegetables with Lime Vinaigrette, 123–25
    Hemp, Kale, and Apple Salad, 126, *127*
    My Veg Lasagna, 152–55, *154*
    Pepperpot Soup, 178–80, *179*
    Spinach Salad with Goat Cheese, Pickled Beets, and Pine Nuts, 133–35, *134*
Spinners, Ital Stew with, 173–74, *175*
Spirulina Smoothie, Cedella's, *92, 93*
split peas, *in* Curry with Ritty Roti, *160,* 161–63
squash, winter
    Ital Stew with Spinners, 173–74, *175*
    Pumpkin Face Scrub, 218, *218*
    Pumpkin-Ginger Donuts, Baked and Glazed, *204,* 205–6
    Saltfish One-Pot, 176–77
star fruit, *in* Catch a Star Juice, *96,* 97

Stew with Spinners, Ital, 173–74, *175*
Sticky Sweet Potato Pudding with Coconut "Conkalonk" Topping, 199–200, *201*
strawberries
    Cedella's Spirulina Smoothie, *92, 93*
    Citrus-Ginger Sorbet with Raise-Up Raspberry Sauce, 194–95
Strong Shine Hair Treatment, 216
sun-dried tomatoes, *in* Guava Ketchup, 114
Superpowered Hemp Dip, 101
sweet potatoes, Japanese
    Pepperpot Soup, 178–80, *179*
    Sticky Sweet Potato Pudding with Coconut "Conkalonk" Topping, 199–200, *201*
Swiss chard, *in* Marley Family Green Juice, 91

T
Taco, Jerk Tofu, with Black Bean–Mango Salsa, 164–66, *165*
Tamarind Barbecue Sauce, Grilled Jerk Chicken with, *140,* 141–42
Tea, Morning Mint, *80,* 83
Tofu Taco, Jerk, with Black Bean–Mango Salsa, 164–66, *165*
tools and equipment, 23
Triple-Threat Spicy Corn Bake, *182,* 183–84
Truffles, Double-Chocolate Brownie, 207–8, *209*

V
Vegetable Broth, Homemade Caribbean-Style, 180
Vegetables, Grilled Jerk, with Lime Vinaigrette, 123–25
Vegetables, Pesto Pasta Stuffed (serving suggestion), 50
veggie burgers (Island Beet Burgers with Avocado and Jerk-Fried Onions), 167–69, *168*
Veg Lasagna, My, 152–55, *154*

W
watermelon, *in* Passion Juice, 95
Wonton Cups, Individual Lasagna (variation), 155

Y
yams, Jamaican yellow
    Pepperpot Soup, 178–80, 179
    Sticky Sweet Potato Pudding with Coconut "Conkalonk" Topping, 199–200, *201*
Yuca Wedges, Smoky Baked, with Guava Ketchup, 114–15

Z
zucchini
    Curry Rundown with Boiled Green Banana, *72,* 73–74
    Grilled Jerk Vegetables with Lime Vinaigrette, 123–25